ISBN 0-933546-49-1
9 780933 546493

KHANIQAHI NIMATULLAHI
(SUFI ORDER)

306 West 11th Street
New York, New York 10014
Tel: 212-924-7739

4021 19th Avenue
San Francisco,
California 94132
Tel: 415-586-1313

4931 MacArthur Blvd. NW
Washington, D.C. 20007
Tel: 202-338-4757

84 Pembroke Street
Boston,
Massachusetts 02118
Tel: 617-536-0076

310 NE 57th Street
Seattle, Washington 98105
Tel: 206-527-5018

11019 Arleta Avenue
Mission Hills,
Los Angeles,
California 91345
Tel: 818-365-2226

4642 North Hermitage
Chicago, Illinois 60640
Tel: 312-561-1616

405 Greg Avenue
Santa Fe, New Mexico 87501
Tel: 505-983-8500

219 Chace Street
Santa Cruz, California 95060
Tel: 408-425-8454

95 Old Lansdowne Road
West Didsbury, Manchester
M20 8NZ, United Kingdom
Tel: 061-434-8857

Kölnerstrasse 176
5000 Köln 90 (Porz)
Federal Republic of Germany
Tel: 49-2203-15390

Van Blankenburgstraat 66b
2517 XS 's-Gravenhage,
The Netherlands
Tel: 070-3450251

50 Rue du 4^{em} Zouaves
Rosny-sous-Bois
Paris, 93110 France
Tel: 48552809

63 Boulevard Latrille
BP 1224 Abidjan,
CIDEX 1 Côte d'Ivoire
Africa
Tel. 225-410510

The Old Windmill
Sulgrave, Banbury,
Oxfordshire OX17 2SH
United Kingdom
Tel: 0295-760361

87A Mullens Street
Balmain, Sydney,
Australia 2041
Tel: 612-555-7546

41 Chepstow Place
London W2 4TS
United Kingdom
Tel: 071-229-0769

The Psychology of Sufism

(*Del wa Nafs*)

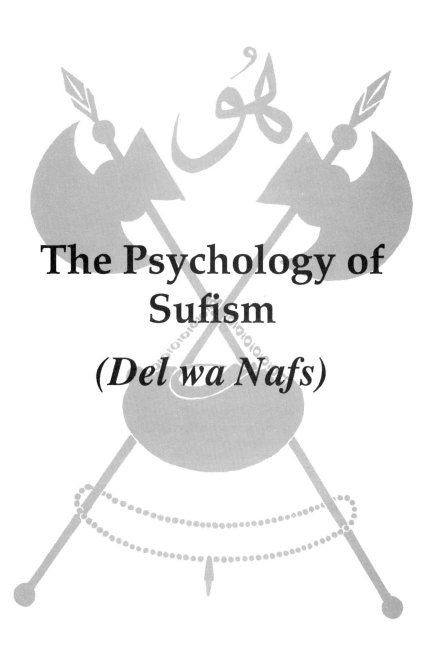

Also available by Dr. Javad Nurbakhsh:

1. In the Tavern of Ruin: Seven Essays on Sufism
2. In the Paradise of the Sufis
3. What the Sufis Say
4. Masters of the Path
5. Divani Nurbakhsh: Sufi Poetry
6. Sufism (I): Meaning, Knowledge and Unity
7. Traditions of the Prophet, Vol. I
8. Sufism (II): Fear and Hope, Contraction and Expansion, Gathering and Dispersion, Intoxication and Sobriety, Annihilation and Subsistence
9. The Truths of Love: Sufi Poetry
10. Sufi Women
11. Traditions of the Prophet, Vol. II
12. Jesus in the Eyes of the Sufis
13. Spiritual Poverty in Sufism
14. Sufism III: Submission, Contentment, Absence, Presence, Intimacy, Awe, Tranquillity, Serenity, Fluctuation, Stability
15. Sufi Symbolism I: Parts of the Beloved's Body, Wine, Music, Samā‘ and Convivial Gatherings
16. The Great Satan, 'Eblis'
17. Sufi Symbolism II: Love, Lover, Beloved
18. Sufism IV: Repentance, Abstinence, Renunciation, Wariness, Humility, Humbleness, Sincerity, Constancy, Courtesy
19. Sufi Symbolism III: Religious Terminology
20. Dogs from the Sufi Point of View
21. Sufism V: Gratitude, Patience, Trust-in-God, Aspiration, Veracity, Zeal, Valour, Altruism, Shame
22. Sufi Symbolism IV: The Natural World
23. Sufi Women: Revised Edition
24. Sufi Symbolism V: Veils and Clothing, Government, Economics and Commerce, Medicine and Healing
25. Sufi Symbolism VI: Titles and Epithets

The Psychology of Sufism

(Del wa Nafs)

A discussion of the stages of progress and development of the Sufi's psyche while on the Sufi Path

BY DR. JAVAD NURBAKHSH

KHANIQAHI-NIMATULLAHI PUBLICATIONS
LONDON NEW YORK

Translated by Terry Graham under the supervision of
Dr. Javad Nurbakhsh in collaboration with
Neil and Sima Johnston.
Designed by Jane Lewisohn
Cover design by Jim Kosinski

Printed in the United Kingdom
On Acid Free Paper

British Library Cataloguing in Publication Data
is available from the British Library
Nurbakhsh, Javad, 1927
The Psychology of Sufism
(Del wa Nafs)

ISBN 0-933546-49-1

Published by Khaniqahi-Nimatullahi Publications (KNP)
41 Chepstow Place
London W2 4TS
England
Telephone: 071-229-0769

CONTENTS

NOTE

al-Nafs: This Arabo-Persian technical term has not been translated due to its wide variety of connotations. Some of its meanings include: essence (of an object), living soul, psyche, spirit, mind, animate being, person, individual, desire, personal identity or self. In Arabic, there are no reflective personal pronouns: their place is supplied by the words *ain* and *nafs* (himself, itself); thus the term *'elm al-nafs* (science of soul) is translated as 'psychology'. Allusion to the term *nafs* in Sufi texts is usually to the *al-nafs al-amarā'*, the lower soul (French: *ame concupiscente;* Latin: *cupido libido),* referring to the human ego which is 'commanded' to evil. In this context the word usually denotes the whole soul-body structure in so far as a man is subject to egocentric ambition and driven by his passions or 'the flesh' (the Greek *sarx* as understood by the Greek Orthodox Christian Fathers). There are also three higher levels to the structure of the soul in its path towards spiritual transformation, viz. *al-nafs al-lawwāma* (the blaming soul or conscience) *al-nafs al-mulhama* (the inspired soul), and *al-nafs al-muṭma'inna* (the soul-at-peace).

TRANSLITERATION EQUIVALENTS

Consonants

Arabic	Latin	Arabic	Latin
ء	’	ض	ḍh(z)
ب	b	ط	ṭ
ت	t	ظ	ẓ
ث	th(s)*	ع	‘
ج	j	غ	gh
ح	ḥ	ف	f
خ	kh	ق	q
د	d	ك	k
ذ	dh(z)	ل	l
ر	r	م	m
ز	z	ن	n
س	s	و	w(v)
ش	sh	ه	h
ص	ṣ	ى	y
		ة	h

Long Vowels

Arabic	Latin
آ	ā
أو	u
اى	i

Short Vowels

Arabic	Latin
اَ	a
اُ	o
اِ	e

Diphthongs

Arabic	Latin
أو	au
أى	ai

Persian Consonants

Arabic	Latin	Arabic	Latin
پ	p	ژ	zh
چ	ch	گ	g

* Letters in parentheses indicate where Persian pronunciation of Arabic letters differs from the Arabic pronunciation.

ABBREIVATIONS

AA	*'Abhar al-āsheqin*
AF	*Aurād al-aḥbāb wa foṣuṣ al-ādāb*
AT	*Asrār at-tauḥid*
EK	*Ensān al kāmel*
ES	*Eṣṭelāḥāt-e aṣ-ṣufiya*
FJ	*Fawāeḥ al-jalāl wa fawāteḥ al-jalāl*
GR	*Golshan-e rāz.*
HAu	*Haft aurang*
KAM	*Kashf al-asrār* (Maibodi)
KF	*Kashshāf eṣṭelāḥāt al-fonun*
KM	*Kashf al-maḥjub*
Lm	*Lama'āt-e Eraqi*
LT	*Loma' fe't-taṣawwof (Ketāb al-)*
M	*Mathnawihā-ye Sanā'i*
MA	*Mashrab al-arwāḥ* (Ruzbehān)
ME	*Merṣād al-'ebād*
MH	*Meṣbāḥ al-hedāya wa meftāḥ al-kefāya*
MM	*Mathnawi-ye ma'nawi*
MN	*Moṣibat-nāma*
NK	*Noṣuṣ al khoṣuṣ*
NN	*Naqd an-noṣuṣ*
RB	*Tafsir-e Ruḥ al-Bayān*
RN	*Resāla-ye Nurbakhsh*
RQ	*Tarjoma-ye resāla-ye Qoshairi*
RQR	*Resālat al-qods* (Ruzbehān)
RSh	*Resālahā-ye Shāh Ne'mato'llāh Wali*
SGR	*Mafātiḥ al-e'jāz fi sharḥ-e Golshan-e rāz.*
SM	*Ṣad Maidān*

SS	*Sharḥ-e shaṭḥiyāt*
TJ	*Ta'rifāt-e Jorjāni*
TKQ	*Tarjoma-ye kalamāt-e qeṣār-e Bābā Ṭāhir*
TSA	*Ṭabaqāt aṣ-ṣufiya* (Anṣāri)
TSS	*Ṭabaqāt aṣ-ṣufiya* (Solami)
TT	*Taṣawwof wa adabiyāt-e taṣawwof* (including *Mer'āt-e 'oshshāq)*

INTRODUCTION

From the Sufi point of view, material nature *(ṭab')*, the self *(nafs)*, heart *(del)*, spirit *(ruḥ)*, the inner consciousness *(serr* or *khafi)*, and the innermost consciousness *(serr-e serr* or *akhfā)*, constitute the stages of advancement through which the human psyche passes on its journey towards perfection.

When one is governed by the *nafs*, one also possesses the characteristics of material nature within one's being. Similarly, when one is governed by the heart, one still possesses vestiges of the *nafs* and material nature within. Those governed by the *nafs* have no awareness of the heart while those governed by the heart have no awareness of the spirit.

> What does the *nafs* know of what is stored in the treasury of the heart? What does the heart know of the subtleties contained in the sanctuary of the spirit? What does the spirit know of the legacy within the pavilion of the inner consciousness? And what does the inner consciousness know of the realities of the innermost consciousness? Indeed, the *nafs* is the site of Divine entrustment *(amānat)* the heart, the house of gnosis, the spirit the sign of witnessing, the inner consciousness, the way-station of love, and the innermost consciousness — only God knows what it holds, and who knows it! It is beyond the imagination of human beings. (KAM VI 112)

According to Sa'di:

> *Perceive the ultimate goal for humanity:*
> *To arrive at a point where nothing is seen*
> *but God.*

Our aim in this book is to review the stages of the psyche's progress from material nature through to the innermost consciousness, giving the views of various masters of the Path on this subject.

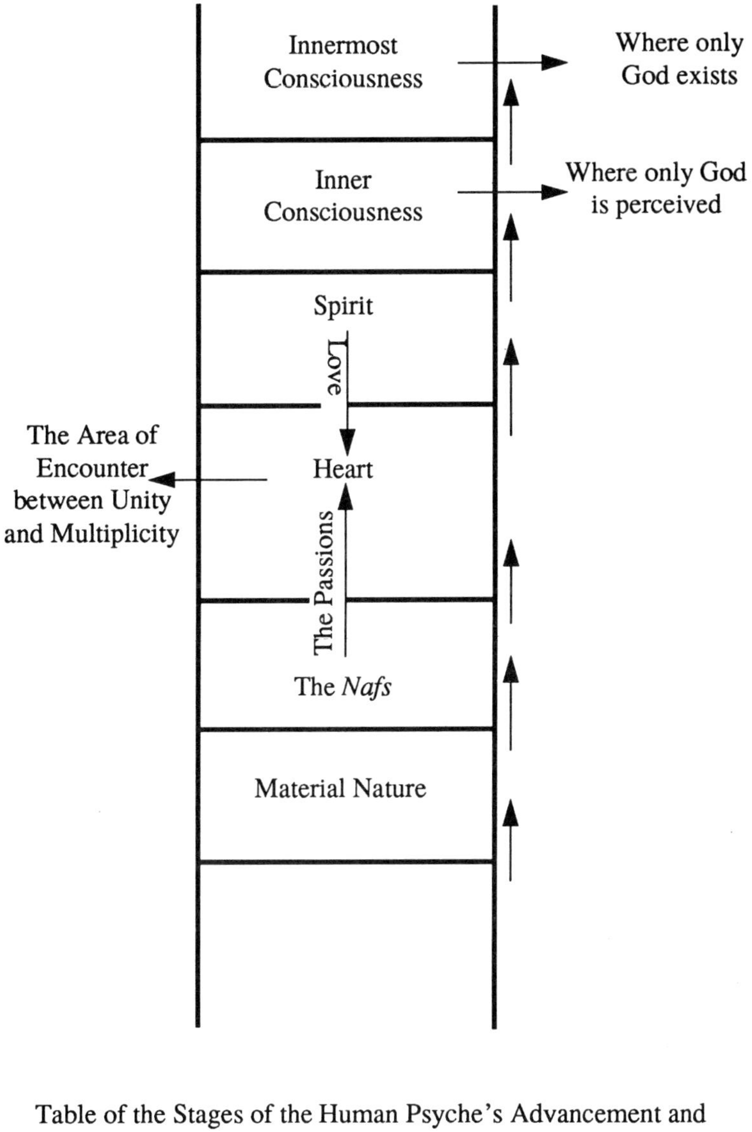

Table of the Stages of the Human Psyche's Advancement and Perfection in the Traversal of the Sufi Path

MATERIAL NATURE

MATERIAL NATURE

The psyche with which a human being is born is known as 'material nature'. Put another way, 'material nature' is the aggregate of psychological faculties with which a human being is endowed at the time of birth; it might be described as the psychological constitution that each individual inherits at birth from his or her parents and ancestors. It should be made clear here that the characteristics of material nature exert an immeasurable influence on the formation of the ***nafs***.

As 'Aṭṭār puts it:

What is material nature?
To plod from one mud-hole to the next,
Like a donkey that repeats its journey
over and over

In Rumi's words:

Have pity on Jesus, not the donkey;
Do not let material nature dominate your
intellect.
Let it weep and wail.
Take from it and give it to your soul.
For years you have been the donkey's slave:
Enough of this, for the slave of the donkey
follows behind it.

MM II 1853 - 55

The Corruption of Material Nature

Abo'l-Ḥasan Sa'egh states, "Wishing and hoping derive from the corruption of material nature."(TA 731)

The Savagery of Material Nature

The material nature of human beings is aggressive and savage, qualities that were inherited from their ancestors and that reside deep in their psyche.

As Sa'di has pointed out:

> *If this savagery should die from your nature,*
> *You will be alive for the rest of your life in*
> *the spirit of human perfection.*

According to Rumi:

> *Material nature seeks vengeance*
> *on the adversary;*
> *Intellect acts as an iron chain upon the* nafs.

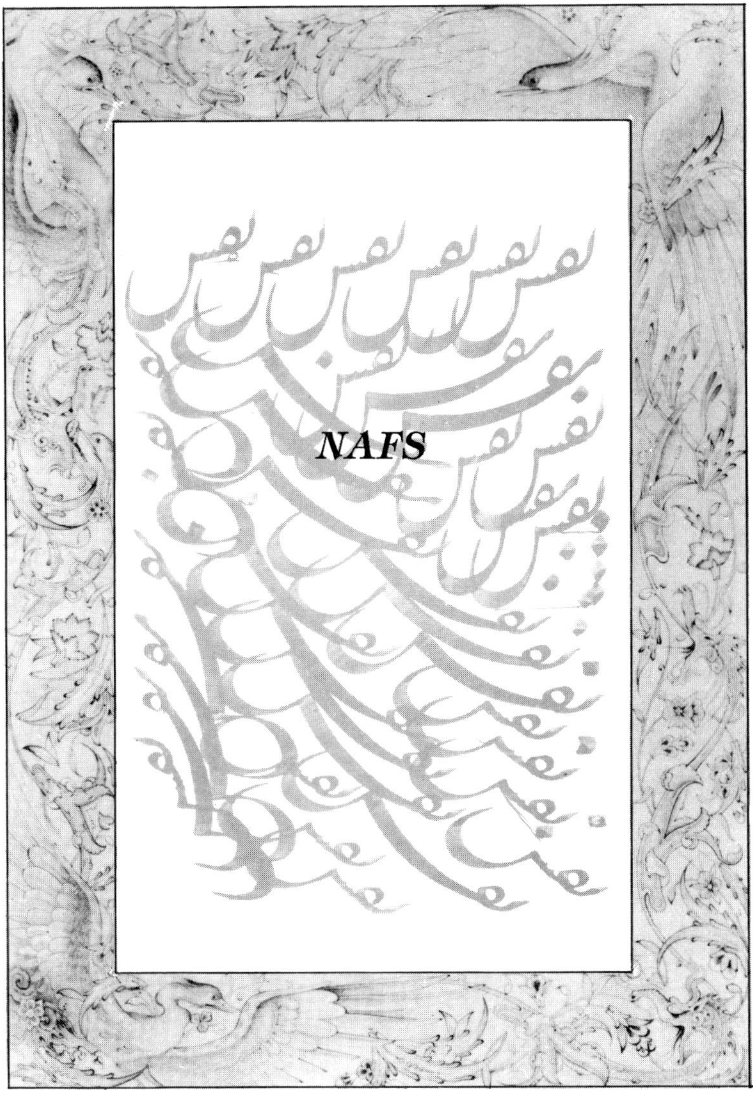

NAFS

NAFS

Material nature is inherited at birth; it subsequently develops into what is termed *nafs* through its encounter with the environment and its exposure to the socialization process in the milieu of family and school. The tendency of the *nafs* is to impose its desires unquestioningly in order to gratify itself. The intellect, however, serves both as a restraining force and counsellor with respect to the *nafs*, advising it as to the positive actions it should perform and the negative ones it should avoid.

In reality, the *nafs* constitutes the ego and its tendencies, while the intellect represents a skillful inspector who attempts to guide the ego in satisfying those tendencies when manifested in society without harming people, channelling the *nafs* into directions that are socially acceptable and, at the same time, beneficial to its state.

All human beings possess *nafs* and utilize it while functioning in society. While certain people are governed by the intellect, the majority are ruled solely by the *nafs*. However, when it comes to the other levels of the psyche, from the heart to ultimate human perfection, the intellect is always at the service of the spirit of perfect humanity.

It should be made clear that the term 'intellect', in this context, refers to the 'particular intellect' *('aql-e jozwi)*, and more fundamentally, to the 'reasoning intellect' *('aql-e estedlāli)*, which serve as the foundation for theosophers and materialist philosophers. The intellect is incapable of knowing Reality for it is constantly changing its views, rejecting each day what it posited the day before.

In this regard Rumi writes:

The legs of those who reason are wooden;
And wooden legs are especially shaky.

At the level of the *nafs*, all persons are more or less equal. The human psyche, however, must pass beyond this stage to that of the heart if it wishes to advance to perfection and knowledge of Reality.

The Attributes of the *Nafs* and the Chastisement Thereof

Whenever the nafs *is suppressed, it reemerges somewhere else.*

Abu Bakr Ṭemestāni said, "The *nafs* is like fire. When at the point of being extinguished, it always flares up somewhere else; if the *nafs* is calmed in one area, it ignites in another." (TSS 499)

'Ali ebn Ṭāleb said, "My state with respect to the *nafs* resembles that of the shepherd with his sheep, where the more he gathers them in one place, the more they scatter in another." (AF 103)

Concepts of the defensive reactions of the psyche, notably Freud's 'displacement reaction' are similar to the example given above.

The nafs *is ignorant*

Abu Ḥamza Baghdādi said, "'Turn away from the ignorant' (VII: 199). The *nafs* is the most ignorant thing of all and the most worthy of rejection." (TSA 99)

The nafs *is the source of base temperament and blameworthy actions.*

According to the Sufis the expressions of a base temperament and blameworthy actions all spring from the *nafs*. The *nafs* has two aspects: the transgressing aspect and that of bad disposition, characterized by pride, jealousy, avarice, ill-temperedness, malice and whatever is reprehensible from the point of view of either the *shari'at* or reason. (KM 246)

The mischief of the nafs is manifested when it is provoked and finds an outlet.

It has been said that the *nafs* is like clear standing water which, when you stir it up, becomes turbid with mud and exudes an unpleasant odor. (AF 103)

The nafs *is the instrument of God's wrath.*

The *nafs* is the instrument of God's wrath; all evil and corruption springs therefrom. The Koran states, "Indeed, the *nafs* commands to evil." (XII: 53) The *nafs* inherently contains the attributes of wrath and is subject to inspiration to do ill, as is described in the Koranic verse God "inspired it [with conscience of] what is wrong for it and [what is] right for it." (XCI: 8) The *nafs* donned the garb of the wrath of the Eternal power and thereby knows God in His aspects of the power of the Might, along with the splendor and the Grandeur.

As the Prophet said, "He who knows his *nafs* knows his Lord."[1]

The gnostic said, "The *nafs* represents the latent aspects of God's inspiration of wrath, its notions being expressed through God's deception *(makr)*." (MA 151)

God created the *nafs*, making it the source of blameworthy temperament and reprehensible actions. He appointed Satan to be the embellisher of the *nafs*. It is like a garden full of plants of all kinds; the seeds sown therein are God's inspiration to do wrong, to flower in the form of fleshly desires and bear the fruit of lust. This occurs when God wishes to test the gnostic at a time when He has granted him insight into his *nafs* through the light of gnosis in the guise of reprehensibility. By the aid of this light and the purity of spiritual striving, he extinguishes the fire thereof. The Koran states, "Say: This is my Way: I call to God with sure knowledge, I and whoever follows me." (XII: 108)

Concerning insight with respect to God, the Prophet said, "Seek a decree from your heart; otherwise, the decreers will issue one to you."

Abu Solaimān said, "I never looked upon the actions of my *nafs* in order to see good in my self."

The gnostic said, "Whoever has vision of God in His wrathful aspect is given insight into the actions of his *nafs*." (MA 155)

The nafs *is like a firebrand.*

The *nafs* is like a firebrand both in its display of beauty and in its hidden potential for destruction; though its color is attractive, it burns.(AF 103)

---

1. See: the authors *Traditions of the Prophet*, vol. II. New York: 1983, p. 45.

When in trouble, the nafs *will seek repentance;*
when in comfort, it turns away from God.

When the *nafs* is being punished, it is zealous in repentance and begs for forgiveness; when comfortable, though, it indulges its passions and turns away from God. (AF 103)

The nafs *is an idol.*

Abu Bakr Wāseṭi said, "The *nafs* is an idol. Looking upon it is idolatry, while reflecting upon it is worship."(AF 103)

The *nafs* is like an idol in the sense that if one looks upon it with desire, one is engaged in idolatry, while if one reflects upon it and learns to gain insight into it, one is effectively engaged in worship.

As Rumi puts it:

The mother of idols is your nafs,
For the ordinary idol is a snake, while this
one is a dragon.

MM I 772

The nafs *finds peace only in deceit.*

Bāyazid said, "The *nafs* is an attribute that becomes tranquil only in deceit; being calmed only by what is other than God, the *nafs* will never submit to the way of God."(KM 251)

The most difficult veil is attraction to the nafs *and adherence to it.*

Dho'n-Nun Meṣri said, "The heaviest of veils is attraction to the *nafs* and its promptings." This is because adherence means being in conflict with God's contentment, and opposition to God is the source of all veils. (KM 250)

As long as the nafs *remains within one, one remains veiled from God.*

Moḥammad ebn Termedhi said, "You want to know God while the vestiges of your *nafs* are still firmly within you, yet your *nafs* does not even know itself; this being the case, how can you know anything at all?" The fact is that one's *nafs*, remaining within oneself, is veiled from itself; how then may God be revealed to it? (KM 251)

The foundation of infidelity lies in fulfilling the desires of the nafs.

Jonaid said, "The foundation of infidelity lies in fulfilling the desires of the *nafs*." That is to say, the basis of infidelity on the part of the devotee is the fulfillment of his bodily desires, for the *nafs* has no connection with the subtle reality of Islam. In fact, it is forever striving to turn away therefrom; and one who turns away denies, and one who denies is a stranger to God. (KM 251)

If the taste of the nafs *is enjoyed,*
the taste of goodness can never be experienced.

Yusof ebn Ḥosain Rāzi wrote to Jonaid, "God did not cause you to enjoy the taste of the *nafs*, for if He had, you would never thereafter have experienced the taste of goodness." (TSA 99)

Latent idolatry is one of the hardest dictates of the nafs.

One of the harshest dictates of the *nafs* is the notion that it is deserving of power over what it possesses; this is considered to be a latent form of idolatry. (RQ 132)

The very constitution (seresht) *of the* nafs *is founded on breach of etiquette.*

Ebn 'Aṭā' said, "The constitution of the *nafs* is founded upon breach of etiquette, whereas the devotee is enjoined to observe etiquette. Thus, the *nafs* by its very constitution opposes God's behest. The devotee should strive to restrain it from seeking to do wrong. If one lets the reins of the *nafs* go slack, one is participating in its bad actions and corruption." (RQ 226)

The nafs *stands accused of evils of all kinds.*

Jonaid said, "This commanding *nafs* is a slave of one who invites it to destructiveness and is an aid to our enemies; it follows its passions and stands accused of evils of all kinds." (RQ 226)

The nafs *always desires that which is prohibited.*

The *nafs* is created in such a way that it desires anything that is forbidden. The secret of this is that it was the *nafs*' primary desire of things that led them to be consequently forbidden." (TKQ 384)

The nafs *is a slave to the passions.*

One of the blameworthy attributes and reprehensible characteristics of the *nafs* is its worship of the passions. It persistently tempts one to indulge in carnal cravings and to seek sensual gratification. It draws to one's side material desires, causing one to comply with the passions. It presents objects of worship other than God to one as indicated in the Koranic passage, "Have you seen the one, who chooses for his god his own passions?" (XXV: 43) This attribute can be removed from the *nafs* only through asceticism and God's love. (MH 85)

The nafs *is a hypocrite, a pretender, and an idolator.*

In most situations, the outward aspect of the *nafs* differs from the inward, and it acts differently in the presence of others than it does in their absence. It praises people in their presence, feigning honesty to their face, while in their absence it does the opposite. This attribute can be removed from the *nafs* only through sincerity. (MH 85)

The nafs *is engaged in adorning itself in a way that pleases people, regardless of the fact that it may displease God.*

The *nafs* is persistently obsessed with presenting itself in such a way as to prompt the good opinion of people, regardless of whether God may disapprove. The result of these actions is the increase of possessions and pride therein, as well as arrogance, self-importance and contempt. It avoids or ignores whatever people disapprove of, even though God may be pleased with these things, for instance, spiritual poverty, neediness and helplessness. This attribute can be removed from the *nafs* only through awareness of one's own contemptibility.

However much the *nafs* makes a show of virtue and attempts to conceal vice, the latter will be hidden only from the short-sighted and the naive, never from those with insight. It is like a hideous old hag who bedecks herself in fancy, dazzling clothes in order to display her finery to children who think the beauty they see is truly hers, whereas those who are mature and aware are made only the more contemptuous. (MH 86)

The deceit of the nafs *has no end.*

Kharaqani said, "I consider all but three things to have their limit: the deceit of the *nafs*, the degrees of the Prophet, and gnosis (of God)." (TA 673)

The nafs *claims divinity.*

The *nafs* always wants people to praise it, to obey moral precepts only as it expounds them, to love it more than anything else. The *nafs* wants others to fear it in all situations, clinging to hope in its mercy, in the same way that God demands these things from His devotees. This position is tantamount to claiming divinity and opposing Divine Lordship. This attribute may be removed from the *nafs* only through theophany of the Divine attributes. (MH 87)

It was in this regard that Jonaid said, "The *nafs* will never find repose in God." (TA 438)

The nafs *is arrogant and egocentric.*

The *nafs* is constantly preoccupied with the virtues of its attributes, contemplating its states with contentment and reverence. It considers important the least thing it has done for anyone, remembering it for years afterwards, being overwhelmed by its own kindness. Yet however great the favors others do for it, it places no importance on them, forgetting them quickly. This attribute of arrogance can be removed from the *nafs* only through awareness of one's own contemptibility. (MH 87)

The nafs *is avaricious* (bakhil) *and depraved.*

Whatever possessions and objects of its desires the *nafs* may obtain, it hangs on to them, refusing to let them go, whether out of greed for more or out of fear of poverty and need. When this attribute gains strength, it spawns envy, and covets the property of others. The *nafs* does not want anyone to receive anything from anybody else, and if it is aware of someone receiving a special boon, it seeks to destroy it. When such envy becomes strong it turns to spite, whereby the *nafs* persistently seeks the destruction of anyone who comes to share in whatever bounty is meted out to it; of those who receive a different amount of a given bounty from it, or who it fears will take away the benefit it has received; or those who might stand in the way of its receipt of some benefit. The attribute of avarice can be removed from the *nafs* only through one's being overwhelmed by the light of certitude. (MH 88)

Why do you complain to God of me,
O knowing one?
Go and complain of the wickedness of the
depraved nafs.

MM II 2717

The nafs *is greedy.*

The *nafs* is constantly and actively engaged in lust and gratification, forever exceeding the limits of moderation. It is insatiable and its greed has been compared to a moth for whom the light of the candle is not enough and which, not dissuaded by awareness of the harm that the heat thereof may cause, hurls itself into the fire and is consumed therein. Moreover, however much the *nafs* may suffer hardship, its craving for pleasure only increases, finally leading to its destruction. This attribute can only be removed through piety and continence. (MH 88)

The nafs *is fickle.*

The *nafs* is never constant. Continually subject to notions and whims, both in word and deed, it sticks with nothing and completes no project, only wanting to finish everything quickly. Its movements are arbitrary and unreliable; it is in a hurry to fulfill its desires, acting precipitously. Certain sages have likened it, in its fickleness to a ball rolling giddily down a slope, constantly in motion. This attribute can only be removed from the *nafs* through patience. (MH 89)

The nafs *quickly becomes weary of all things.*

The *nafs* soon wearies of things. Its false view is such that it seeks to rid itself of the task of the moment finding repose only in occupying itself with the next task, not realizing that it will never gain respite in this manner. In most cases, the actual matter turns out differently from what it desires. If, by any chance, the *nafs* should succeed in attaining what it wants, it will still not be satisfied. The *nafs* needs stability. One can be rid of this affliction only by performing one's duties sincerely. (MH 89)

The nafs *is indolent.*

Just as the *nafs* is fickle and in a rush to attain what it desires, it also hurries through its devotions and good works out of indolence and laxity. This infirmity of the *nafs* can be removed only through intense ascetic discipline and rigorous spiritual striving to dislodge the inner contraction and frigidity which is the basis of its disobedience and recalcitrance. By bringing about the acceptance of injunction and compliance with commands, this discipline softens the *nafs*, as tanning does to hides, as indicated in the Koran, "their flesh and their hearts soften to God's reminder." (XXXIX: 23) (MH 89)

The nafs *changes its color at every moment.*

The *nafs* is like a chameleon, changing color moment by moment, and hourly changing shape. It is the angel Hārut of Babylon in one's being, constantly engaged in fruitless activity, every moment up to mischief of one kind or another. (MH 83)

The nafs *is oblivious, unforgiving, and resentful.*

If the *nafs*, after years of receiving affection, should happen to be subject to unkindness on one occasion, it will be oblivious to all the beneficence it has enjoyed, becoming upset and resentful at the single unkindness, which it cannot forgive. In its expression of this characteristic, the *nafs* is lower than many animals.

The nafs *likes to be complemented and praised by others.*

The *nafs* likes praise. It continually enjoins a person to put on pretensions, so that people will compliment it. Indeed, there are worshippers and ascetics enough who are thus at the command of the *nafs*.

One of the latent vices and secret maladies of the *nafs* is its love of praise. Whoever imbibes a draught of it will move the seven heavens and the seven sublunar realms for the very flutter of an eyelash. The symptom of this affliction is that when the *nafs* is deprived of praise, it falls into indolence and laxity.

For years a certain master would do his prayers in the front rank in the mosque. One morning something prevented him from making the early prayer on time, so he had to stand in the back row. After this he stopped coming to the mosque altogether. When he was asked about his absence, he replied, "For years I had been performing my prayers under the impression that I was sincere. The day I had to stand in the back row, I was struck with shame, realizing I had simply been taking pleasure in being gazed upon by the people. From that time I approached my prayers properly." (RQ 149)

The nafs *sometimes takes pleasure in worship.*

Sometimes the *nafs* enjoins one to prayers, fasting and the Pilgrimage, not, though, for the sake of obeying the *shari'at,* but rather for the sake of its own pleasure and profit. For example, the *nafs* enjoins one to undertake the Pilgrimage so people will call one a 'pilgrim', whereby one can deceive them all the better.

If the nafs *bids you to pray and fast,*
It is deceiving you and
hatching a plot against you.
MM II 2274

Morta'esh said, "I undertook several pilgrimages in detachment from the world. I then discovered that this was all for the gratification of the *nafs* when my mother one day told me to bring her a pitcher of water from the well. That was very hard for me. I realized then that I was following my *nafs* in undertaking those Pilgrimages. I had completed them solely for the sake of pleasing my *nafs*. If had I been annihilated from the *nafs*, I would not have found it difficult to carry out what the *shari'at* made incumbent upon me [fulfilling my mother's request]." (RQ 150)

The nafs *is more hostile than any enemy.*

On the basis of the Prophet's statement, "Your *nafs* is more hostile than your enemy, for it lies within you," the Sufis consider the *nafs* to be more dangerous to a person than any foe and are emphatic about being wary of it.

There is no tyrant that is more of an enemy
For the wayfarer than the commanding nafs.
You cannot face the qebla, *nor can you turn*
left or right.

On your right lies the garden of the Unseen;
On your left stands that of deception.
In between these two lies the
innately hostile nafs,
Always sitting there.
Whatever is bestowed from left or right
And is free of flaw or imperfection,
The nafs *discards through greed and lust,*
Or pollutes with conceit and hypocrisy.
Everything that exists, whether human
or otherwise,
Either flees in accord with God's will or
complies in deed and speech.
However, this wicked, ill-favored nafs,
Which holds you in a single embrace,
Cannot be avoided through prudence,
Or be evaded through subterfuge.
Neither kindness nor malice will extricate
you from it;
This is the secret of, "There is no enemy
more hostile..."

HAu 36

The nafs *may sometimes be inactive like a dragon frozen by the cold.*

Inactivity freezes the *nafs*, which becomes inactive when deprived of opportunity, or space and time, for displaying itself. Nevertheless, whenever it finds a suitable milieu, it will awaken and spring into action, creating trouble and turmoil in the process.
According to Rumi:

A snake-hunter went to the mountains to trap
a snake
Through his incantations.
He searched the mountains during the time
of the snow
To find a great strong snake.
In hunting for snakes in the harshness of
winter
The snake-hunter discovered a huge dead
dragon,
Whose size was such that it filled his heart
with fear.
The hunter then picked up that dragon
And brought it to Baghdad in order to aston-
ish the people.
"I have brought a dead dragon!" he cried.

"I suffered greatly in hunting it down."
That man thought it was dead
but it was alive,
Though he was not aware of this.
It had been made dormant by the cold and snow;
Although alive, it appeared to be dead.
The man displayed it on the bank of the river,
And a furor arose in the town of Baghdad.
Hundreds of simpletons gathered there, having become
Prey to him as he to the dragon through his folly.
Hundreds of fools gathered around
Pressing around in a circle.
That dragon which was motionless
Was now buried under hundreds of rags.
That keeper had taken precautions
And had tied it up with thick ropes.
In the time lapse between expectation and event,
The sun of Iraq shone forth upon that snake.
The tropical sun warmed it up;
The cold humors left its limbs.
Though it seemed dead, it came alive;
Bewildered, the dragon began to uncoil.
As that dead snake stirred, the people's amazement
Multiplied a hundred thousand times over.
Terrified they began to scream.
They stampeded, fleeing its movement.
It had broken its bonds and burst forth,
A hideous dragon, roaring like a lion.
In the rout many people were killed;
A hundred piles were made from those that fell dead.
The snake-hunter froze in fear on the spot,
Muttering, "What have I brought from mountain and plain?"
The dragon ate up that confounded man in a single gulp.
Such savagery is easy for that which is a bloody tyrant.
Your nafs *is such a dragon: how can it be dead?*
It is merely frozen due to lack of means.
Were it to obtain the means of Pharaoh,

At whose command the Nile would flow,
It would do things in the manner of Pharaoh
And waylay a hundred Moses and Aarons.
Keep the dragon in the snow of separation
from its desires;
Beware, do not transport it into the sunshine
of Iraq!
Let that dragon of yours remain dormant.
Should it be released it will devour you.
Do you aspire, without the use of force,
To keep it bound in dignity and fidelity?
This wish cannot be enacted by any old rub-
bish;
It requires a Moses to slay such a dragon!
Because of
the snake-hunter's plan
hundreds of people were killed
By that deceiving dragon.

MM III 977-1066

The Decree of the Nafs.

Abu Bakr Wāseṭi said, "Any prompting that harbors the slightest appeal to one's self-interest, or attaches one in any way to the world, is a decree of the *nafs*. The *nafs* prompts one in knowledgeable language in order to beguile one, whereby one may subsequently deceive others, as is indicated in the Koranic passage, "Layer upon layer of darkness." (XXIV: 40) (TA 738)

Infidelity of the Nafs

Ruzbehān gives a particularly interesting account of the *nafs*' infidelity:

The *nafs*' infidelity falls into three categories: with respect to miraculous powers, with respect to states, and with respect to visionary revelation.

Infidelity with respect to miraculous powers concerns the manifestation of God in the realm of action, such as the transmutation of principal essences *(a'yān-e thābeta),* where created beings cannot comprehend God's signs and miracles and become agitated, doubting these with a disposition characterized by ignorance and blindness which causes misgivings. No matter how many signs, major and minor, may be shown to such a *nafs*, it would still not become a believer. Indeed, because of the apparent domination of the *nafs* by the spirit, and its chastisement by the heart, and the constant flow of God's bounties to the gnostic, the *nafs* deceptively appears to be in repose. However, it can never be intimate with the heart. There is no conciliation between us and it, for created being can never enjoy intimacy with it. Hence, in creating *nafs* God diverted its attention away from His Being to its own existence, such that were it able to be conscious of God, it would never have disbelieved in Him. However, it sees only itself, and is therefore blind to God.

This is the infidelity of Pharaoh, who saw only himself and was blind to God, whence he became an infidel, for when one looks at God through oneself, seeing God through one's own eyes it is infidelity to God's Attributes. When one sees God through God, it is infidelity to one's own attributes. The latter is the basis of Divine Unity, whereas the former is the foundation of infidelity. Sometimes it happens that one's entire being is *nafs*, and sometimes one's entire being is soul. Whenever one looks at oneself through oneself, one is wholly *nafs*, whereas whenever one looks at God through God, one is completely soul.

The *nafs*' infidelity in spiritual states is such that, when the self-praising *nafs* of the gnostic enters the origin of love, it finds the pure wine of subsistence filled with the joy of the Holy Grandeur. The soul of soul drinks the wine of Lordship with the savor of devotion, from the cup of soul. Free of nature it moves in nature, and as it does so it cries out ecstatically, overwhelmed by love and from every particle of the being of that liberated one a tongue cries out, "I am God!". The disbelieving *nafs*, at this point, confronts the gnostic crying, "You are not God!" It says this because it cannot know God, for this knowledge only occurs through God, and whoever denies this is an infidel.

Infidelity with respect to visionary revelation occurs when the veils before the Divine Presence are lifted, and the brides of Reality appear. Divine forms appear to the rational spirit *(ruḥ-e nāṭeqa)* as sacred spirits thereby displaying themselves to pure spirit. The wonders of the realm of dominion appear from the marvels of the Unseen. The soul maintains that this is Divine Unity, while the infidel maintains that it is fantasy *(tashbih)*, for his temperament is imagination, perceiving the angelic realm through the eye of imagination. He ridicules this, not understanding that these are wonders of Lordship manifested in the sources of devotion. The *nafs* does not adhere to Divine Unity, because it dwells in multiplicity. The soul adheres to Divine Unity, because it does not originate in the material world. Therefore it is a believer in God's marvels. (RQR 81)

The Reactions of the Nafs.

In order to indulge its passions, the *nafs* ignores rules, religious regulations, covenants, etiquette or social conventions; that is, it wants its lustful desires and motives and innate demands to be obeyed unquestioningly. Because of these qualities, blocking the desires of the *nafs* will stimulate mental conflicts, engender anxiety, depression, nervous conditions, and many irrational forms of behavior.

Visions (ro'yāt) *of the* Nafs.

Visions of the *nafs* appear when one is conscious of the realm of God's wrath, for whoever knows God's wrath knows the quality of his *nafs*. Ruzbehān writes about visions of the *nafs* as follows:

> Whenever God wishes to acquaint His devotee with the deceptions of the *nafs*, He presents them in the form of blameworthy traits to make him aware of the *nafs* and its defects and how they may be remedied, so that he may become liberated from the evil of the *nafs*, whereby he comes to know God through what He presents in the guise of wrath.
>
> The Prophet said, "Whoever knows himself knows his Lord."
>
> The gnostic said, "Appearence visions of the *nafs* means consciousness of the realm of wrath." (MA 274)

Ruzbehān considers 'visions of the *nafs*' to be a station of the chosen and writes:

> When the *nafs* finds tranquility through drinking at the wellsprings of the heart that are fed by the springs of the spirit, which in turn flow from the streams of the Attributes, which pour from the rivers of the Acts, the lights of the Attributes are unveiled for the spirit and the heart. The *nafs* views the brides of God's Acts in the imaginal realms, finding repose therein, and takes pleasure in the company of the heart and spirit. Accordingly, the *nafs* is made tranquil by command of the heart, the intellect and the spirit. However, when the *nafs* becomes turbid and dominates the intellect, imprisoning it, God presents its lustful tendencies and secret deviations to itself in the wrathful form of satanic fantasies. Testimony to this matter is embodied in the Koran, where it

> tells us that God, "...inspired it [the *nafs*] with conscience of what is wrong for it and what is right for it." (XCI: 8)
>
> The gnostic said, "Visions of the *nafs* are to behold the wrath of pre-eternity." (MA 126)

Ruzbehān further describes 'visions of the *nafs*' as a station of lovers, writing:

> Whenever the *nafs* is severed from its lusts, it seeks the pleasure of dealing with God and the resultant benefits thereof. Since the *nafs* traverses the path of devotion in the company of the heart, and the heart controls the *nafs* with the reins of its own annihilation in the wrath of the Divine Lord, the lights of the illumination of pre-eternal characteristics are revealed to the *nafs*. The heart annihilates the *nafs* from the desire for all that is other than God such that, from the heavens to the earth, nothing remains for the *nafs* but God. This level is not attained by the *nafs* either through direct observation or the imaginal realm. Nevertheless, it is still subject to the force of wrath from the Unseen. This is something which only a few of the gnostics comprehend.
>
> The Prophet referred to his own particular condition when he said, "My Satan has become a Moslem."
>
> The gnostic said, "Visions of the *nafs* are revealed to the eye of the heart where the decrees of the angelic realm become manifest."(MA 170)

The Gnosis of the Nafs.

The gnosis of the *nafs* is dependent on awareness of the Divine Acts, the realities of Divine deception, and the root and origin thereof. Ruzbehān explains this in the following way:

> Gnosis of the ordinary is that of the outward acts of the *nafs*, which oppose the *shari'at* and the Path. Gnosis of the elect is that of the subtleties, realities, and deceptions of the *nafs*, freeing the spirit thereby to soar to the realm of Divinity. The gnosis of the elect is that of the existence of the *nafs*, its points of entry and exit, and the knowledge that the *nafs* is the cloak of accusation woven in the workshop of Divine wrath, allowing the beauty of the grandeur to display itself while remaining disguised to the adherents of Divine Unity so that they may never know God through all His Attributes. The eye, which sees through this dis-

guise, receives the light of vision from the eye of perfection, such that it sees the source of wrath through the eye of grace. Where is the teacher who knows the beast through these defects, to provide disciples with a shield to ward off affliction and sincere ones with the sword of contentment? (RQR 79)

The Tradition, "He Who Knows His Nafs *Knows His Lord"*[1] *Interpreted.*

In the context of this tradition, there are two meanings of the word *nafs*: one as *nafs* as has been discussed above, the other as 'self'.

If we consider the first meaning of the *nafs,* it has two interpretations: one being that whenever one comes to know one's *nafs* one will know God's wrath; the other being that whenever one comes to know one's *nafs* one realizes that most of the apparent instances of experiencing the Lord have in fact been merely the experience of one's *nafs*, not God. In this sense the key point lies in the rendering of the word *Rabb,* which must be translated as 'guide' rather than 'Lord'.

The definition of *nafs* with respect to the passions and blameworthy desires is relatively easy. Defining it in terms of its deceptive guise is not so simple, for the *nafs* may, for example, command one to be a worshipper, an ascetic, a savant or a Sufi, solely for the purpose of being accepted by people, of being respected and praised by others.

The *nafs* may even assume the guise of visionary revelation *(kashf),* contemplative vision *(shohud)* or miraculous power *(kerāmāt)* in order that the gnostic might worship himself rather than devote himself to the worship of God.

From this brief explanation, it should be clear to most people that the 'guide' and 'inspirer' is really their *nafs*, although they are not aware of this at the time.

When the *nafs* is interpreted to mean 'self', the Tradition reads, "He who knows his self knows his Lord." In this sense, it may be interpreted thus: whenever one comes to know oneself to be needy, one will know one's Lord to be free of need, or whenever one comes to know oneself through annihilation, one will know one's Lord in subsistence.

As Jonaid said, "Whoever knows himself as helpless knows his

1. See: *Traditions*, p. 45.

Lord as all-powerful, and whoever knows himself in error knows his Lord as merciful." (TSA 637)

Abu Sa'id Abe'l Khair said, "When one comes to know oneself to be non-existent, one comes to know one's Lord as All-existent." (AT 319)

It has also been said that whoever knows himself to be abject knows his Lord to be Almighty, or whoever knows himself in servanthood knows his Lord in Lordship. (KM 247)

Symbolism of the Nafs *in Dreams.*

There are many ways in which the *nafs* may be symbolized in dreams, the forms varying according to the negative characteristics which dominate a particular *nafs*. There are as many symbolic representations of the *nafs* as there are Sufis who travel the Path. However, the most common symbolic representations of the *nafs* in dreams are: the snake, dog, wolf, rat, monkey, bear, donkey, or an old hag.

If the prime characteristic of the *nafs* is aggression and violence to others, the *nafs* may be represented in dreams in the form of a snake. If deception and trickery are the dominant traits, the representation may be of a fox or an old hag. If anger and viciousness predominate, a dog or wolf may appear. If greed and covetousness of property and provision dominate, a rat might be the symbol. If lust and sensuality are dominant, a monkey, bear, or donkey may be seen. Finally, if egocentricity and self-love rule, then one may observe an individual resembling oneself.

A number of prominent Sufis have commented upon the symbolic aspects of the *nafs*, some of which are reported in Hojwiri's *Kashf al-maḥjub*:

Abu 'Ali Siāh Marwzi recounted, "I once saw my *nafs* in a form resembling my own. Someone had seized its hair and given it to me. I tied it to a tree with the intention of destroying it, when it cried, 'O Abu 'Ali, do not take the trouble! I am God's army; you cannot destroy me.'"

An eminent companion of Jonaid, Moḥammad 'Olyān Nasawi, is reported to have said, "In the early stages of the Path, I gained insight into the evil effects of the *nafs* and became acquainted with its places of ambush. I harbored a constant hatred of it in my heart. One day, something like a fox-cub leapt out of my throat, which, through God's grace, I recognized to be my *nafs*. I trampled it underfoot, yet every time I kicked it, it grew bigger. I asked it why, since other things are destroyed by such treatment. It replied, 'Because I was created perverse: whatever bothers others comforts me, and vice versa.'"

Abo'l-'Abbās Ashqāni, the Imam of the time, recounted, "One day, I came home and found a yellow dog lying there, asleep. Thinking it had come in from the neighborhood, I was just about to turn it out when it slipped under my cloak and disappeared."

Abo'l-Qāsem Gorgāni (Karrakāni) said, "I once saw the *nafs* in the form of a snake."

A dervish reported, "I saw my *nafs* in the form of a rat. I asked, 'Who are you?' It replied, 'I am the destruction of the heedless for I incite them to wickedness. I am the salvation of the friends-of-God, for if it were not for me and my diseased existence, they would be proud of their purity and their actions. When they contemplate their purity of heart and inner consciousness, the light of their friendship with God, and their constancy in spiritual practice, they become proud. Through this, they see me in themselves, and as a result all their pride disappears.'" (KM 259)

Human Manifestations of Material Nature and the Nafs.

Ordinary people are manifestations of material nature, kings, of the *nafs*, philosophers of the intellect, and prophets and friends-of-God of God. (RSh I 342)

The Passions of the Nafs

The passions *(hawā)* form a part of the conscious side of one's *nafs* of which they are considered to be a catalyst. They reinforce the ego, and go hand in hand with the *nafs*. It is through these passions that the *nafs* finds fulfillment of its desires.

The passions constitute the *nafs*' desire for that which gives gratification and brings satisfaction. At the same time, the passions divert the *nafs* from what it despises, regardless of religious principles, social conventions, the etiquette and customs of society.

Both passions and intellect attract the *nafs*. If the intellect dominates, the result is advancement and spiritual progress. If the passions dominate, the consequence is bestial actions, deviation, and destruction.

> 'Ali ebn Sahl Eṣfahāni said, "The intellect and the passions are in conflict with each other. Spiritual success is the handmaiden of the intellect, spiritual failure that of the passions. The *nafs* lies between these two, serving whichever of the two prevails."
> (TSS 232)

From the above, it is clear that the passions of the *nafs* obstruct progress on the path and the process of perfecting the *nafs*. The *nafs*, in turn, obstructs the heart's advancement. Through these obstructions, one is held back from the traversal of higher stations.

The Different Kinds of Passions.

The passions of the *nafs* are too extensive to delineate here. They have, however, been divided into two general categories: those that relate to the seeking of pleasure and the indulgence of lust, and those that motivate ambition, selfishness, and the desire for power.

> The passions are of two kinds: the desire for pleasure and lust, and the desire for rank and authority. Those who follow the former haunt taverns and therefore generally represent no danger for people. Those who seek religious rank and authority, however, live in cloisters and monasteries, and as such represent a threat to humanity, for they have deviated from the path and lead others astray. We take refuge in God from those who follow the passions.
>
> Those whose entire conduct is motivated by their passions, and who find fulfillment through pursuit of them, are far from God. Those who have cut themselves off from the passions and renounced the pursuit of them are close to God, even though they may be in an idol temple.
>
> Ebrāhim Khawwāṣ said, "When I heard that there was a man in Rum who had spent seventy years in a monastery in ascetic rigor, I thought to myself, 'Amazing! The term of monastic commitment is normally forty years. What noble purpose has kept this man in a monastery for seventy years?' I set out to find him. When I finally approached the monastery, a window opened and this very man called out to me, 'O Ebrāhim, I know why you have come. I have not remained here for these seventy years for the sake of monastic commitment. Rather, I have a dog here who is agitated with its passions. I sit here watching over this dog to keep it from bothering people. I am not what you imagine!' On hearing these words, I exclaimed, 'O Lord, You are able to guide a devotee in righteousness even while he is completely astray and confer the right way upon him.' He chided me, saying, 'O Ebrahim, how long will you continue to seek out people? Go seek yourself, and when you have found yourself, keep watch over yourself, for every day these passions don three hundred and sixty garments of divinity and lead you astray.'" (KM 261)

The Passions and Anger.

Certain Sufi masters consider desire and renunciation as characteristics of passion, while other eminent Sufis, such as Najmo'd-Din Rāzi, maintain that attraction is a characteristic of passion and repulsion a characteristic of anger, both being attributes of the *nafs*.

The *nafs* has two characteristics: the passions and anger. The passions represent desire and intentions directed towards that which is base, while anger represents willfulness, arrogance, and the tendency to dominate.

The attribute of the passions is used to attract benefit to oneself, while that of anger to repulse harm. A balance must be struck between these two attributes, for deficiency in either causes a deficiency in the *nafs* and body, while excess in either causes deficiency in reason and faith. The cultivation and purification of the *nafs* will bring the two characteristics to a state of moderation.

If the passions exceed the limits of moderation, then mischief, greed, expectation, meanness, baseness, lust, avarice, and treachery will appear. Moderating the passions involves the attraction of the sort of benefit that answers one's needs as they appear, while if one desires more than what is required, one will become corrupt. If one desires benefit before experiencing need, greed arises. If one desires the benefit for long life, expectation arises. If one desires something base and shallow, then baseness and meanness result. If one craves high rank and pleasure, then lust arises. If one wishes to own things, avarice results. If one is afraid that in spending, poverty will result, then bad intentions occur.

If the characteristic of the passions is recessive and deficient in an individual's nature, then flaccidity, impotence, and abjectness result.

If the characteristic of anger exceeds the limits of moderation, then bad disposition, arrogance, rancor, irascibility, quick-temperedness, intolerance, tyranny, instability, falsity, conceit, vanity, willfulness, and selfishness arise. If one cannot expel one's anger, resentment takes root in one's inner being. If the characteristic of anger is deficient and recessive within an individual, then self-contempt, flaccidity, indifference, infirmity, depravity, and incapacity result. If both passion and anger are dominant in an individual, envy results, for domination of the passions causes one to covet everything one sees in others in order to bring pleasure to oneself. Domination of anger causes dislike of someone who possesses things that one does not possess oneself. Thus, envy is the product of desiring something that another owns and not wanting anyone else to own that thing.

When these characteristics dominate the *nafs* completely, the very constitution of the *nafs* is inclined towards vileness, iniquity, murder, pillage, harassment, and corruption.

The philosophers have erred in that they have not understood that the attributes of the passions and anger, as well as lust and all other blameworthy characteristics associated with these two, cannot be completely eliminated. They themselves have labored to eliminate these characteristics for years and still have not succeeded. Rather than accept the existence of imperfection, from which other blameworthy characteristics arise, they seek to deny the passions and in so doing bring about flaccidity, impotence, abjectness and baseness of aspiration. Similarly, in seeking to deny anger, they encourage self-contempt, weakness in religion, indifference, infirmity, and cowardice.

The virtue of the *shari'at,* and the alchemy of religion, is that these attributes are confined within the limits of moderation, each being utilized in its appropriate domain. Religion works in such a way as to dominate these characteristics, restraining the *nafs* from going its own way, reining it in like a horse, rather than allowing these characteristics to dominate the individual and carry him along like a captive, like a wild horse that bucks and throws itself and its rider uncontrollably into a pit, or against a wall, both becoming destroyed in the process.

Thus, whenever the attributes of the passions and anger are balanced through the elixir of the *shari'at,* and pious practice, the *nafs* can manipulate them only by command of the *shari'at,* and through this, praiseworthy attributes will appear. When the attributes of shame, generosity, munificence, courage, clemency, humility, manliness, satisfaction, patience, gratitude, and other praiseworthy qualities appear, the *nafs* becomes transformed from the station of 'commanding' into that of 'rest', becoming the lead camel of the pure in spirit. In traversing the way-stations and stages of the Path, from the lower degrees to the higher, like Borāq (the steed that conveyed the Prophet on his Journey of Ascent), the *nafs* carries the spirit through the sublime levels of the empyrean and of 'two bows length', after which it becomes worthy of these words of God, "Return to your Lord, content in His good pleasure." (LXXXIX: 28)

The spirit needs the Borāq of the *nafs* on its journey of ascent to its domain, for it cannot go by foot. It enters this realm mounted on the steed of God's breath, as indicated in the Koran, "I breathed into him of My Spirit." (XV: 29 & XXXVIII: 72) At this point in its journey to the new realm, the spirit needs the

Buraq of the *nafs* in order to reach the limits of the *nafs*, which in turn needs the two characteristics, the passions and anger, if it desires to travel higher, or indeed, if it seeks to go back down.

The masters of the Path have observed in this context: "No one can travel the Path to God without the passions," the reason for this being that the passions and anger are like Nimrod's two vultures, such that whenever the *nafs* mounts them it is carried high toward its prey. In this way, these vultures direct themselves upward, and bear the lowly *nafs* to the sublime stations.

When the *nafs*-at-rest is in control of the passions and anger, and acquires the taste for God's words, "Return to your Lord, contenting, contented," it turns the passions and anger away from what is lower, and looks to what is higher, such that nearness to the plane of the Might becomes its aim, not the pleasures of the bestial realm below. Once the passions have set their sights upward, they turn entirely into love and loving-kindness. When anger directs its attention upward, it becomes entirely caring and full of aspiration. It is love and loving-kindness that focus the *nafs* on the Divine presence, and it is care and aspiration that carry it from station to station without stopping or looking back, its concentration directed toward the plane of the Might. These two instruments thus serve as the most complete means for the spirit's attainment of the Divine presence.

Prior to arriving in the Divine presence, the *nafs* came to the realm of the spirits where it had no need of these two instruments, being, like the angels, content with its station, and content in witnessing the radiant light of the candle of the majesty of Oneness, as where an angel says, "There is not one of us but has his known station." (XXXVII: 164) It lacked the boldness to advance beyond this station. Like Gabriel, it said, "If I came closer I would be burned." However, like the spirit, the *nafs* became acquainted with the earth; and through its coupling with the elements, the spirit produced the *nafs*, from which, in turn, sprang the two offspring, the passions and anger. The passions are the ultimate ignorance and anger the ultimate oppression. When the *nafs* looked downward, these two—the utterly ignorant and the oppressive—drove it to destruction. The spirit was also under their control at this level; thus all were subject to destruction.

Through blessed fortune, the wild horse of the *nafs* was lassoed by the attraction of, "Return to your Lord, contenting, contented," calling it to the sublime realm and the plane of Might.

When that rider, the spirit, attained its 'known station', it wanted, like Gabriel, to rein in the steed. That wild horse of a *nafs*, like a mad moth, driven by its two wings, the ignorant passions and oppressive anger, hurled itself upon the candle of Oneness. It renounced figurative existence and became united with the candle which transmuted its moth-like figurative being into its own candle-like True Being.

The *nafs* cannot be considered perfect until it has brought its ignorant and oppressive handiwork to perfection, for who is it, and for what reason was it created? What work at what station did it come to seek? When this handiwork is completed and its moth-like madness attains the candle-like emanation of light, in the manner of the Prophetic Tradition, "I become the ears with which he hears, the eyes with which he sees, the tongue with which he speaks,..." the reality of "Whoever knows his *nafs* knows his Lord," is realized. This is to say that whoever comes to know the *nafs* as a moth, will come to know the Divine presence as a candle. (ME 178)

The Passions and Satan.

From the Sufi point of view, Satan is none other than the amalgam of the attributes of the *nafs* which arise from the realm of Wrath. In other words, Satan is the manifestation of God's Wrath.

Satan can find a place in the devotee's inward being only when the desire to sin occurs within him. When but a hint of the passions appear, Satan snaps it up, embellishes it, and displays it to the devotee's heart. This is what is generally called 'temptation' and all temptation begins with the passions, as it is said, "The instigator is the worst oppressor." This is the meaning of God's answer, "Indeed, as for My servants, you have no power over them," (XV: 42) when Eblis said, "By Your Might, I shall lead all of them astray." Thus, Satan is connected to the reality of the *nafs* and the passions. The Prophet referred to this when he said, "There is no one who has not been taken over by his Satan except 'Omar, who has managed to conquer his Satan." (KM 262)

Resisting the Passions.

The Masters of the Path have urged that the passions be resisted. This involves preparatory work which will be explained further below. It is interesting to note that in Sufi terminology the word *hawā* (passions) has two meanings: one, that of the passions of the *nafs*, and the other, that of God's love. This indicates that whoever enjoys God's love is blind to his own passions.

> Renunciation of the passions gives the disciple control over them; indulgence in them makes him subject to their domination. When Zolaikhā indulged her passions, she gave up control and became subject to them, while Joseph, in renouncing his passions, broke their control and became the controller.
>
> When Jonaid was asked the meaning of Divine Union, he replied, "Renouncing indulgence of the passions."
>
> Whoever seeks grace through Union with God must resist the passions, for no spiritual practice is greater than this; tearing down a mountain with one's fingernails is easier than resisting the passions.
>
> Among the anecdotes of Dho'n-Nun Meṣri is the following: "I saw someone flying through the air and asked him how he had attained such a degree. He replied, 'I trampled on the passions and found myself in the air.'"
>
> Moḥammad ebno'l-Faḍhl of Balkh said, "I am amazed at those who go to visit God's House (Mecca) carried by their passions. Why do they not just stamp them out so that they may attain God and behold Him directly?" (KM 263)

Lust.

The most extreme pleasure-seeking aspect of the passions of the *nafs* is lust. Inasmuch as the attraction of pleasure has different aspects, there are various forms of lust: sexual lust, lust for status and power, lust for wealth, and so forth.

Rumi considers lust to be antagonistic to the intellect:

Intellect is the opposite of lust, O brave one;
Do not ascribe lust to that which is the
intellect.

MM IV 2301

Show me one who is a man at the moment of
lust and anger;
I run from street to street in search of such a
man.

MM V 2893

Hojwiri on Lust.

The most obvious attribute of the *nafs* is lust, which is dispersed throughout the human body, all senses being subject to its influence. It is incumbent upon the devout to protect all parts of his body from it for he will be held to account for the actions of each part. The lust of the eye is sight, that of the ear, hearing, that of the nose, smell, that of the tongue, speech, that of the palate, taste, that of the limbs, touch, and that of the mind, thought. Hence the seeker must be his own keeper and governor, and spend day and night throughout his life keeping watch. He must cut out of himself the incitements of the passions that appear in the senses, and appeal to God to transform his lustful attributes in such a way that his desires are eliminated from his inner being. Whoever is afflicted by the sea of lust is veiled from all spiritual realities. Accordingly, if the devotee should seek to drive lust out from himself by his own efforts, the task will be a long one, for lust will constantly recur in different forms. Such an aim may be achieved only once he has submitted to God. (KM 263)

Ruzbehān on Lust.

A Sacred Tradition from God, spoken by the Prophet, states, "The more My servant busies himself with Me, the more I will turn his lust toward communion with me." The lust of the lover appears only in love and in the desire to behold God's Beauty. It is something special in the lover, and occurs solely in the contemplation of God's Beauty; however, contemplation of the Grandeur and the Splendor burns away the lust of love.

Jonaid said, "Contemplation of the Splendor and the Grandeur causes intimacy to fall away from the hearts of God's friends."

The gnostic said, "Human lust is the steed of spiritual lust, which is, in turn, the steed of the lust of love; and the lust of the lovers is the longing experienced by spirits for the realm of joy in spiritual things." (MA 136)

Definitions of Lust by Masters of the Path.

Hātem Aṣamm said, "Lust is of three categories: that of eating, speaking, and seeing. In eating one should maintain one's confidence in God; in speaking, one should maintain truth; and in seeing, one should maintain wariness [of God's warnings]. (TA 302)

Jonaid said, "Lust serves as an indication of the *nafs*, and frivolity indicates infidelity. (TA 440)

Rowaim said, "Lust remains concealed until ready for action." (TA 486)

Ebn 'Aṭa' said, "The heart, the spirit, and the *nafs* each possess a different kind of lust, but all are gathered together in the individual. The lust of the heart is in beholding God, that of the spirit in being close to Him, and that of the *nafs* in enjoying ease." (TA 492)

Subjection to the Nafs' *Control.*

The great expounders of the Path have vigorously warned against heeding the *nafs*, pursuing its promptings, and observing its desires, as the following passages demonstrate.

One who heeds the promptings of the *nafs* falls prey to pride. (TKQ 384)

Jonaid said, "Infidelity is founded on observing the desires of the *nafs*." Inasmuch as the *nafs* can never be in harmony with the subtle nature of Islam, being unable to concentrate thereon, it will finally deny Islam; and one who denies is an alien. (KM 251)

Dho'n-Nun Meṣri said, "The heaviest of veils is subjection to the *nafs* and obedience to its command. When one yields to the command of the *nafs*, one is opposing God's contentment. Opposition to God is the foundation of all veils." (KM 250)

In the course of a sea voyage, Sohrawardi
Presented me with two bits of advice.
One, not to be suspicious in company,
The other, not to be subject to the nafs.
Sa'di

Controlling the Nafs.

Sufi masters consider success on the Path to derive from control of the *nafs*.

According to a Prophetic Tradition, the powerful one is not he who conquers people, but one who succeeds in conquering his *nafs*. (MH 85)

He who is controlled by the *nafs*, must serve it.; he who controls the *nafs* serves others. (TKQ 599)

He who does not rely on his *nafs* becomes humble. (TKQ 385)

Freedom from the Influence of Nafs.

To be free of the influence of *nafs* is to be free of the temperament of the *nafs*, the attributes of which are anger, irritability, arrogance, avarice, greed, and envy. If the devotee remains sound with respect to such traits, forbidding them to arise within him, he becomes free of the *nafs*' influence, and appears to have no *nafs* at all.

Abu Sa'id Kharrāz said, "The devoted one who returns to God becomes attached to Him and finds repose in nearness to Him, forgetting his *nafs* and everything that is other than God." Thus, if anyone asks with whom he associates, he has no reply but to say, "God," for, because of the veneration for God in his heart, he knows no other." (LT 360)

The Falling Away of the Nafs.

When the lights of the Grandeur and the Splendor, and the reality of Lordship and servanthood, overwhelm the Pole but do not annihilate his *nafs* therein, he perceives his *nafs* to be the worst kind of infidelity.

The gnostic said, "Whenever reality of Divinity becomes manifest, the sincere one sees his *nafs* as being valueless before other *nafs* and all other things. (MA 309)

Resistance to the Nafs.

One way to train the *nafs* is to resist its desires. However, if we wish to resist, we know that we must not resist by opposing or suppressing it, for when we do, it will rear up somewhere else, seeking gratification of its desires. Thus, it has been said that to resist the *nafs* through the *nafs* is an error. (TKQ 542)

Statements of the Masters of the Path Concerning Resistance to the Nafs.

Resistance to the *nafs* is the basis of all spiritual practice and the perfection of all spiritual endeavor. Only through this can the devotee find the way to God, for conformity with the *nafs* is destruction for the devotee, while resistance to it is salvation.

God has enjoined all to resist the *nafs*, praising those who strive to do so and condemning those who allow themselves to conform to it. (KM 246)

Abu Solaimān Dārāni said, "The best of all activities is to resist the *nafs*, for it betrays its trust and is a barrier to seeking God's contentment." (KM 251)

Abu Ḥafṣ [Ḥaddād] said, "Unless you condemn your *nafs*, resisting it at every moment and in every situation, and deny yourself even that which is permissible, you will be constantly deceived by it. If you are content with your *nafs*, you will be destroyed; how could a wise man be content with this?"

The Koran reports Joseph as saying, "And I do not exonerate myself. Indeed the *nafs* enjoins one to evil." (XII: 53) (RQ 226)

Anecdotes Concerning Resistance to the Nafs

Jonaid recounted, "One night I could not sleep, so I got up to complete my litanies. I experienced none of the sweetness normally accompanying this. Trying again to sleep, I could not. Trying to sit, I grew restless. I opened the door and went out. In the street I saw a man wrapping a coarse cloak around himself and when he saw me he turned and called out, 'O Abo'l-Qaṣem, come here!' I asked what for. He replied, 'Indeed, I was appealing to the Mover of hearts to move your heart for my sake.' I then asked, 'What is your problem?' He answered, 'How can the sickness of a sick man become his cure?' I said, 'His sickness can become his cure through resisting the *nafs*.' He then addressed his body, saying, 'Listen body! I answered you seven times and you did not accept. Now, listen to Jonaid!' Then he turned away and left. I had no idea who he was." (RQ 226)

Ebrāhim ebn Shaibān is reported to have said, "For forty years I spent not one night in privacy, or in any place that had been locked up. Once, I experienced a desire for lentils. After having eaten them, I then went out for a walk in the street. While walking I noticed a shop with bottles hanging on display. I thought they were filled with vinegar, but someone told me they were filled with wine, and that there were more casks of wine there as well. I was suddenly overcome with the desire to go into the shop and empty the bottles and casks, which I did. The vintner thought I was doing this on the orders of the king. When he realized that

I was doing this of my own volition, however, he grabbed me and dragged me to the Ebn Ṭulun mosque, where he ordered me to be beaten two hundred times after which I was thrown into prison. I spent some time there, until my master, Abu 'Abde'llah Maghrebi, came to town and interceded for me. When he saw me, he asked what I had done. I told him of my desire for the lentils and how I had eaten them, and how I had been beaten two hundred times. He then told me that I had been lucky and had gotten off lightly. (RQ 228)

Ebrāhim Khawwāṣ said, "Once, on my way to Mount Lokām, I came upon a pomegranate tree, the fruit of which I immediately craved. I picked one, broke it open, and found it to be bitter. I threw it away and continued my journey. Along the way, I saw a man lying prostrate with bees swarming all over him. When I greeted him, he responded by calling my name.

I asked how he knew me, and he replied, 'Nothing is hidden from one who knows God.' In response, I said, 'I see that you are in a state with God. If you like, God can protect you from those bees and relieve you of their stinging.' He replied, 'I see you too are in a state with God. If you appeal to Him, he will relieve you of the desire for pomegranate, for biting the pomegranate leads to pain in the hereafter, whereas the pain of the bite of the bee is experienced in this world.' I left him and continued my journey. (RQ 227)

Ja'far Naṣir recounted, "Jonaid gave me a dirham to buy vaziri figs. I bought them and brought them to him. When he broke his fast, he took one and put it in his mouth, then took it out, began crying, and told me to take them away. I asked him why, and he said that a voice had come to his heart, saying, 'Have you no shame? You gave this up for Our sake, yet now you desire it again.'"(RQ 229)

Combat with the Nafs

The term *mojahada* means 'to strive' or to 'wage combat'. In Sufi terminology, it signifies 'combat with the *nafs*' through controlling the desires of the *nafs* and transforming its blameworthy characteristics into praiseworthy ones. Sufi masters have placed special emphasis on 'combat with the *nafs*' for those who have newly entered upon the Path, and maintain that unless this combat is waged from the beginning, nothing will be achieved on the Path.

For the ordinary devotee, 'combat with the *nafs*' involves observation of spiritual practice and resistance to the appetites of the *nafs*; for the elect, it involves the conversion of the characteristics of the *nafs* into human qualities and Divine attributes.

'Combat with the *nafs*' must be waged for the sake of God, not in the hope of visions or miraculous powers. Emam Ja'far Ṣādeq said, "He who wages combat with the *nafs* for the sake of the *nafs* may acquire miraculous powers, but one who does so for God, attains God."

> The Prophet said, "The combatant is one who wages war with his *nafs* for the sake of God," and, "We have returned from the lesser combat *(al-jehādato'l-asghar)* to the greater combat *(al-jehādato'l-akbar)*." When asked what the greater combat signified he replied, "combat with the *nafs*."
>
> The Prophet considered combat with the *nafs* nobler than combat on the field, for the battle is a more difficult one. Know, then, that combat with the passions and victory over the *nafs* is a momentous and glorious endeavor.
>
> Sahl ebn 'Abde'llāh Tostari placed great emphasis on spiritual combat, saying, "Witnessing is the result of spiritual combat." Others have said that the Prophet did not suggest that everyone who battled with the *nafs* attained God through grace, for grace has nothing to do with effort. They maintain that the objective of spiritual combat is to discipline the *nafs*, not to attain nearness to God. Inasmuch as spiritual combat involves the devotee's effort and may result in the grace of witnessing, it is absurd to think that one should necessarily bring about the other.
>
> To substantiate his view, Sahl cites the Koranic passage, "As for those who wage combat through Us, We guide them unto Our ways." (XL:29) He argues that to deny the role of spiritual combat in the attainment of God does not mean the denial of spiritual combat itself, but rather self-consciousness of spiritual combat, such that one should not be pleased with one's actions when involved in the sacred domain. Spiritual striving is an act of the devotee while witnessing arises from God's grace. Without God's grace, the devotee's actions have no value. Thus, the spiritual combat of the friends of God is that of God Himself working involuntarily through them, such that they are overwhelmed thereby and dissolved therein, the act of dissolution being grace itself. Spiritual endeavor which is oblivious to God indicates action for the sake of itself; the volition thereof amounts to agitation and dispersion, where the heart becomes distracted and itself dispersed. Hence, the devotee should try as hard as possible not to be conscious of his actions and not to fol-

low the *nafs* under any condition, for the existence of his individual being is his veil. (KM 251 & 257)

Abu 'Ali Daqqāq said, "When one embellishes one's outward being with spiritual endeavour, God embellishes one's inward being with witnessing," and also, "If at the beginning one cannot rise, at the end one will not be able to sit."

Abu 'Ali 'Othmān Maghrebi said, "You are mistaken to think that the door to Reality will be opened through anything but spiritual endeavour."

Bāyazid said, "For twelve years I was the blacksmith of my *nafs*. For five years I was the mirror of my heart, and for one year I gazed into that mirror and saw a cincture around my waist reflected there. For twelve years I was thus engaged until finally I cut myself free. After this, I gazed further into my inward being and saw a cincture there as well, and for five years I contemplated how I might cut it. When this was revealed to me and I looked upon people, I saw them as dead and repeated *'Allāho akbar'* four times."

Sari Saqaṭi said, "O young people, do youthful things now, rather than wait for old age like me when you will be too weak to do them." Needless to say, no youth could equal Sari in his worship, even at this stage of his life.

Abo'l-Ḥasan Kharrāz said, "This work is founded on three things: eating only in time of need, sleeping only when overwhelmed by need, and speaking only when necessary."

Ebrāhim Adham said, "One may attain the station of the virtuous only by undergoing six disciplines: do not take pleasure in bounties, but subject oneself to rigor; do not think well of oneself, but abase oneself; do not consider oneself self-sufficient, but humble oneself in indigence; do not satiate oneself, but go hungry; do not sleep, but stay awake; and do not hope, but await death."

Know that the essence of spiritual combat is renunciation of the pleasurable habits of the *nafs*. One must oppose the *nafs* at all times. The *nafs* has two characteristics: heedless lust, and rebellion against worship. When the steed of the passions of the *nafs* rebels, one needs the bridle of piety. When it is headstrong in its refusal to conform to God, one needs the whip of opposition to the *nafs*, and when it arises in anger, one must be kind to it, for there is no greater victory than one achieved through kindness, for kindness quenches the fire of anger with temperance. When the wine of wantonness becomes sweet for the *nafs*, it can only be made content through adoration and indulgence in whatever it may desire. In order to break this state, one must make the *nafs* endure pain and abasement until it knows the baseness of its nature. Ordinary spiritual combat is vigorously waged in action, while that of the elect is waged in purifying states, so that hunger and wakefulness become easy for one, and bad temperament turns to good. All of these things are difficult. (RQ 146)

Whenever the disciple constantly contemplates that which God has deemed necessary for him, he wages combat against the *nafs* until it passes away through refinement, thereby allowing the heart to live through the light of remembrance. He closes the doors of the heart to the passions and the desires of his *nafs*. He digs lust and doubt out of the field of contemplation of God, so that the terrain of the heart, once a salt-marsh, may become fertile, allowing the seeds of love to be sown, cultivated and purified in the soil of remembrance. The disciple tends and irrigates this plant with the water of purity and protects it from destruction by sudden plagues, thereby encouraging it to grow with the light of the sun of the Might and the shade of the moon of witnessing. Through this care, the branches grow into the air of eternity and the roots take a firm hold in the soil of sanctity.

The Koran states, "Its root set firm and its branches reaching into heaven." (XIV: 24)

The Prophet said, "We have returned from the lesser combat to the greater."[1]

The gnostic said, "The gnostic's spiritual combat is to maintain his lofty aspiration and keep it safe from relapse into the baseness of material nature." (MA 20)

Mortification (riāḍhat) *of the* Nafs.

'Mortification of the *nafs*' arises from enduring hardship and disappointment in order to purify the *nafs*. It is customary for Sufi masters to ask their novice disciples to do things that do not appeal to their *nafs*, so that their being and their egocentricity may be broken, and their *nafs* mellowed and calmed from wantonness and rebellion.

---

1. See: *Traditions*, vol. I, p. 77.

'Mortification' is the purification of the *nafs*' temperament. Purification of the *nafs* is to cleanse it of its material nature and the desires associated with it. (TJ 151)

'Mortification of the *nafs*' is to break, through service, the power of the *nafs*, and to ensure that the performance of service is maintained at all times. (TA 578)

In view of the above points, Sufi masters required their novice disciples to eat and sleep only when necessary, and to perform actions difficult for their *nafs*, the purpose of which was to strengthen their resolution and control of the *nafs*.

Destruction of the Nafs.

When Sufis speak of the destruction of the *nafs*, in the context of controlling it, they use the expression 'annihilation of the *nafs*'. This signifies the annihilation of those characteristics associated with the *nafs* and their transformation into qualities associated with a true human being. The *nafs* itself, however, is indestructible, for it is simply the lower level of the psyche, the elementary level of development. When Sufis say that 'so-and-so' has no *nafs*, they mean that the characteristics of that person's *nafs* have been transmuted into positive human qualities, such that no trace of the *nafs* remains visible in them.

One who was aware said:
Destruction of the nafs *means destruction of*
its ugly nature.

Aṭṭār

Abu Bakr Ṣaidalāni said, "The only real life is through the death of the *nafs*, whereby the heart comes alive." He further stated, "It is impossible to destroy the *nafs* through the *nafs*. This may be accomplished only through God, and even that may be realized only through devotion to God." He also said, "The greatest blessing is to destroy the *nafs*, for it is the greatest veil between you and God. There is no attainment of Reality without the death of the *nafs*." (TA 721)

Bāyazid said, "When one causes the *nafs* to die, one becomes wrapped in the shroud of God's mercy and interred in the earth of His ennoblement. When one causes one's heart to die, one becomes wrapped in the shroud of God's curse and buried in the earth of His punishment." (MH 84)

> God created the commanding *nafs (nafs-e ammāra)* in a state of resistance to Him, for it seeks from its Master, God, Lordship and this is not granted to it. Thus, God has commanded that eternity slay the *nafs*, so that nothing but God may exist in the confines of the heart and that adherence to Divine Unity may be detached from anything other than God. The destruction of the *nafs* can come about only through seeking God's help and taking refuge in Him, for the sea of love surges through the mystery of God's theophany and can annihilate the *nafs* through the first overpowering burst of the light of gnosis. Thus, when the *nafs* and its passions become annihilated, God causes signs and miraculous powers to appear to the gnostic.
>
> The Koran states, "And God gave him [David] the kingdom and wisdom and taught him that which He wills." (II: 251)
>
> The gnostic said, "Destroying the *nafs* can only be accomplished through gnosis of God, which leads to knowledge of the *nafs*." (MA 194)

The Nafs *and Satan*

Certain Sufi masters have considered the *nafs* and Satan to be two separate things, while others have deemed them to be the same, describing them as two bodies in one spirit.

> Those who view the two as being separate maintain that two enemies of religion exist, towards whom hostility is necessary: Satan and the commanding *nafs*. They consider the latter to be harsher than Satan, for Satan does not covet the believer's faith, but demands only transgression from him. The *nafs*, however, attracts the believer to infidelity, and demands infidelity of him. Satan flees the power of God, while the *nafs* stands firm.
> (KM 153)

> Those who view Satan and the *nafs* as the same thing maintain that Satan is in fact the *nafs* as well as the passions of the devotee. The Prophet said, "There is no one whom Satan has not overthrown, except 'Omar, who has mastered his passions," thereby implying that the two are the same. (KM 262)

As indicated in the following quatrain, Rumi considers Satan and the *nafs* to be two forms with the same essence:

The nafs *and Satan have ever been one;*
They have manifested themselves in
two forms.

MM III 4053

Is Satan the Human Personality?

One must realize that the passions serve as the driving force behind the actions of the *nafs*, and the ego serves as the force behind the actions of the personality. The passions are controlled by the *nafs*, and the ego is controlled by both the *nafs* and the intellect. Whenever the *nafs* wishes to gratify the passions, the Satanic ego seeks help from the intellect, and directs the way in which the *nafs* should act in order that it should not be discovered and put to shame. The ego, or Satan, does not covet a person's faith, for that is influenced by the intellect, and the *nafs* has nothing to do with the intellect, being concerned only with attracting a person towards transgression and infidelity. Following the intellect as it does, the ego flees from God's power, whereas the *nafs* itself claims to be God, and as such, has no fear of Him. Whoever maintains that Satan and the *nafs* are the same is correct, inasmuch as the ego is part of the *nafs*. After all, it was 'Omar's lack of ego to which the Prophet referred when he said that he had overcome his Satan.

The ego, with the help of the *nafs* and the intellect, motivates the ordinary person towards egocentricity, whereas in the case of a person of heart, the ego is under the influence of the heart, being, for all intents and purposes, totally incapacitated thereby. It is in this context that it has been said the greatest veil between a person and God is one's very being and egocentricity, for which Satan was driven from God's court.

Ḥallāj's Ecstatic Statement Concerning the Nafs

Ḥallāj ecstatically stated, "The gnostic's ladder is his *nafs*. His essence is the gateway to Union with God's Essence." In expounding upon this statement, Ruzbehān states:

> "Here the *nafs* of the gnostic is the site of spiritual combat from which there is a ladder leading to the heart, which is, in turn, the threshold of the gateway to the spirit. When one begins to climb the ladder of spiritual combat, one enters the gateway of the heart. In entering the realm of the heart, one discovers that the spirit has become one's essence. Once the spirit has been attained, one has reached the gate to Union with the Eternal.

Whoever crosses these seas is saved by the ships of devotion from the sea of transitiveness, whereupon one witnesses the Eternal. The Koran speaks of the one who, '...restrained his *nafs* from the passions: Indeed, paradise will be his refuge.'" (LXXIX: 40-41) (SS 394)

The Involuntary Obedience To God of the Gnostic's Nafs

Whenever the spirit gains intimacy with God, its pleasure becomes shared by the *nafs*, such that the *nafs* obeys the spirit, for whatever pleasure the *nafs* desires from spiritual practice is acquired through the spirit.

The gnostic said, "Whenever the *nafs* finds repose in increased ecstasy, and derives pleasure therefrom, it gains serenity and engages in spiritual practice without any strain whatsoever." (MA 296)

Exhorting the Nafs

Everyone must open the book of inspiration before one's *nafs*, in order to remind it of its Primal Source, so that it will focus its attention on the attributes of the passions and desires through the realm of lights, for God has placed a spiritual reality in each *nafs* that motivates it to move towards its Origin. The *nafs* however, rejects whatever represents the Divine Origin and the praiseworthy attributes which are manifested in the body of this spiritual reality. This is a spiritual reality that God has placed in trust in the divinely related *nafs* so that His pre-eternal power and everlasting and impenetrable force may be manifest and spread through His grace emanating therefrom. This spiritual reality is pledged to its disciples as a means to know God. When God removes this means, only the source of the individual essence remains for the *nafs*. This is a spiritual reality that is particular to the *nafs* of a gnostic, for the gnostic consecrates servanthood specifically because he has been pre-eternally chosen for his pure, undefiled love, a love without motive. According to the Koran, "He loves them and they love Him." (V: 54)

The gnostic experiences this love after witnessing the Might and hearing the message of Union. Subsequently, God causes the witnessing of Himself to be realized for the gnostic, after which he acquaints the gnostic with His Essence, unveiled and without the intermediary question, "Am I not your Lord?" (VII: 172) Once the flight from this source has ended, the gnostic remains on the path of devotion and retains the natural attributes of human nature. One who still possesses *nafs* must remind the *nafs* of the signs and guidance provided by the source of the Divinity, so that it does not turn away from the sublime sources. In this regard, the Koran speaks of "a reminder for those of understanding." (XXXVIII: 43 & XL: 54)

The Prophet said, "Remember death constantly."

The gnostic said, "Exhortation of the *nafs* involves the encouragement of good conduct in spiritual practice, and the yearning of the spirit for witnessing."(MA 27)

Cleansing of the Nafs

Cleansing of the *nafs* consists of three things: giving thanks rather than making complaint, being alert rather than heedless, and being sober rather than drunk. (KAM V 727)

Training the Nafs

Training the *nafs* basically involves resistance to it and its demands. This resistance cannot be undertaken by the *nafs* itself, for resistance to it might simply arise from its desire to attain a greater gratification of its appetites. For example, a person governed by the *nafs* might reject a delicious dish of food simply for the sake of a more delicious dish, or be encouraged to reject it by the *nafs*, rather than by God. Similarly, there are those who are commanded by the *nafs* to perform all sorts of rigorous disciplines and undertake severe asceticism solely for the purpose of performing extraordinary feats.

Occasionally, in order to make up for the reprehensible things it has done, the *nafs* may unconsciously encourage a person to learn the science of religion. The real motive behind this, however, is for that person to win the admiration of others, that is, to have his hand kissed, to be seated at the head of public gatherings, to be honored and celebrated by others, thereby gratifying the *nafs*.

The principles on which the Sufis have based the training of the *nafs* are founded on the renunciation of self-love and the dedication to love of that which is other than the self. This is aptly expressed in the following verse:

Do not be content, like a dog, with sleeping
and eating;
Even if you are confronted by a cat, give
your heart to it.

This foundation of love, the friendship for others, arises from devotion to the master and Divine love, that, when realized, leads to the following fruitful results:

Devotion to the master engenders the Sufis preference for the master's contentment over that of the *nafs*, thus reducing attention to the *nafs* and its desires. It also causes the energy of the *nafs* to be expended in service to the master and the desire to fulfill the master's wishes, such that the force of the *nafs* becomes weakened thereby.

> *Nothing will slay the* nafs *but the aegis of the master;*
> *Grasp tightly the skirts of that slayer of* nafs.

Devotion to the master also leads the disciple unconsciously to identify with him and strive to assume his attributes. The master is selfless, free of desire, and graced with God's temperament, and it is through identification with him that the disciple becomes refined.

Devotion to the master makes easy the Sufi's acceptance of the master's instructions which oppose the desires of the *nafs*.

Continuous attention to God causes remembrance of God which drives awareness of other things out of one's consciousness, causing the desires of the *nafs* to become gradually forgotten.

Continuous attention to God engenders the gradual transmutation of the attributes of the disciples' *nafs* into the Attributes of God.

> *So long did he sit before my susceptible heart*
> *That the heart completely absorbed his temperament and qualities.*

As a result of the above factors, delight of spirit and heart comes to the *nafs*, without its conscious involvement. This arises from its intimacy with God, such that the *nafs* discovers repose and obedience in the constant flow of promptings to the heart and spirit. Ultimately, Divine love causes the Sufi to suppress the *nafs* and its characteristics, the ego and its desires, and the doubting intellect, whereby it gives away all that it possesses to the fervor of love, and alienates itself from all that is other than the Beloved.

The Stages of the *Nafs*

Most Sufis maintain that the *nafs* comprises four levels: the commanding *nafs (nafs-e ammāra)*, the blaming *nafs (nafs-e lawwāma)*, the inspired *nafs*, *(nafs-e molhama)*, and the *nafs*-at-rest *(nafs-e moṭma'enna)*.

The natural substance of the commanding *nafs* is fire, that of the blaming *nafs* air, that of the inspired *nafs* water, and that of the *nafs*-at-rest earth.

The Commanding Nafs

The commanding *nafs*, or that which commands one to commit evil, constitutes the *nafs* of the ordinary person. This is the *nafs* that has not been purified and refined, it is the source of all evils; it conforms in its actions with all that is wrathful and domineering. The Sufis have derived this term from the Koranic verse, "Indeed, the *nafs* commands one to evil, except that whereupon my Lord has mercy." (XII: 53)

Below are a few of the statements made by masters of the Path concerning the commanding *nafs*:

The commanding *nafs* is that which has not passed through the crucible of ascetic discipline, or shed the tough hide of existence. It actively resists all of God's creation. This *nafs* is of a bestial character that harasses other created beings and constantly sings its own praises. It always follows its own desires and grazes in the field of material nature; it drinks from the spring of the passions and knows only how to sleep, eat, and gratify itself. It is human in form, but Satanic in nature, confirming the statement that 'Satans' may be of both 'human' and 'jinn' substance. It is a mighty veil which covers religion and serves as the source of corruption and the focus of evil. (KAM V 92)

The commanding *nafs* enjoins a person to evil and invites him to the sites of self-destruction that God has appointed for His enemies. Those who pursue the passions of the *nafs* are drowned in affliction and characterized by all kinds of wickedness.
(MH 85)

The commanding *nafs* encourages one toward corporeal nature and encourages sensual pleasures and lust. It drags the heart down and is the refuge for evil and the source of a blameworthy temperament. (TJ 312)

The *nafs* commands one to acquire an evil nature because of its own innate material nature. Whenever one yields to it, only evil can result, for it enjoins only to evil. However, whenever its Lord has mercy on it and casts a favorable glance upon it, He releases it from its own innate nature and transmutes its attributes by transforming its domineering aspect into compliance and its wickedness into goodness. (RB IV 275)

The commanding nature of the *nafs* exists behind the veil of material nature and as such has yet to acquire that awareness of God, the Creator and Source of itself that would enable it to return to its Lord, as indicated in the Koranic verse, "Then unto Us is their return," (X: 70) Because of this lack of awareness, the commanding *nafs* seeks only worldly, sensual, and illusory pleasure, its aspirations being confined to the satisfaction of these ends. (MD 232)

In the early stages of the Path, as long as one is under the control and domination of the *nafs*, it is known as the commanding *nafs*. In these circumstances, where the *nafs* is still rooted firmly in material nature, it constantly seeks to drag the spirit and the heart down from a higher to lower level, namely, to its own established level. It constantly presents itself as an adorned object of adoration to others, while Satan stands by to further embellish its beauty in order to attract other spirits and hearts, thereby bringing the lofty spirit low, and defiling the pure heart with trickery. (MH 84)

The commanding *nafs* has ten attributes: ignorance, anger, rancor, tyranny, arrogance, spite, envy, avarice, infidelity and hypocrisy; hence, it is the centre of all defilement and evil.

The commanding nafs debases you:
If you are aware of this do not give it your
respect.

Sa'di

You enter the hell of the commanding *nafs* only when God wishes to acquaint you with it and its temperament, and make you aware of it, so that you may come to know Him as the Creator, as indicated by the words of Joseph, His sincere one, when he said, "Indeed, the *nafs* commands you to evil," (XII: 53) and through His own words, "We shall show them our signs on the horizons and in their *nafs*, until it is made clear to them that it is the Truth."

The Prophet said, "One who knows one's *nafs*, knows one's Lord."

The gnostic said, "One who knows one's *nafs* in annihilation knows one's Lord in subsistence." (MA 15)

The Deceiving and the Bewitching Nafs

In the *Kashf al-asrār,* Maibodi discusses two kinds of *nafs*: the 'deceiving' and the 'bewitching', each of which is actually an aspect of the commanding *nafs*.

The deceiving *nafs* is lower than the commanding *nafs*, in that it lacks the power to resist a person's will. However, it is constantly seeking an opportunity inwardly to ambush the unsuspecting person. For example, when it sees a disciple engaged in spiritual endeavor and asceticism, and in a station of concentration, it presents him with the idea of making a devotional journey, a pilgrimage, or a visit to a shrine, or to fight a holy war. When it says that such activity is a higher level of devotion, it speaks the truth in the general sense. However, in this case, it is merely a deception, a ruse presented for the purpose of turning the disciple away from his station of concentration so that his thoughts will be distracted and he will be thrown into confusion, thus making it difficult to attain the goal. Even if the disciple were to be successful in resisting any of the above, he would never experience that station of concentration again.

On the Path of devotion, it is necessary for disciples to have a master, for the master knows all the waystations of the Path, and all potential traps set by the deceiving *nafs*. He is able to analyze the disciples' states and guide their thoughts through that which accords with their efforts. The great Sufis have maintained that one must gain serenity in order to be safe from the wiles of the deceiving *nafs*. (KAM V 93)

The bewitching *nafs* haunts the adherent to Reality. If one is firm in one's devotion and ascetic discipline, then one's *nafs* begins to plead for sympathy and begs that one takes pity on its poor state. If the adherent is not aware, it drags him down from the station of Reality to that of the *Shari'at*. It tempts him to take license thereby, encouraging him to indulge himself, thus satisfying the *nafs* and strengthening its hold over him until the adherent of Reality drops back to the first step and allows the commanding *nafs* to once again lead the way.

> The bewitching *nafs* does not lead to sin; rather, it leads to devotion as one embarks upon the Path, bewitching the unsuspecting, saying, "You are far better than the corrupt drunkard." If this is believed, and one considers oneself superior, one will be led to destruction. (KAM V 93 & 94)

The blaming nafs

The blaming *nafs* is known as such because it chastises itself for its own bad actions. The term, blaming *nafs*, is derived by the Sufis, from the Koranic verse, "Nay, I swear by the blaming *nafs*." (LXXV: 2) Concerning the 'blaming *nafs*' Sufi masters have made insightful statements, some of which are quoted below.

> Whenever the morn of guidance dawns in the night of human nature, lighting up the sky above the horizon of the heart, the *nafs* turns to its blaming aspect, chiding itself for its own bad actions. Becoming remorseful for the evil it has committed because of its commanding aspect, it repents before God.
> (RB IV 275)

> When the commanding *nafs* is purged of most of its sickness through God's favor and the influence of a perfect and perfecting master, what remains of it is transformed into the blaming *nafs*. In other words, when the commanding *nafs* adheres to the heart, it surrenders, but as long as attributes of the *nafs* linger, they will continue to blame themselves for their shortcomings. (RSh 347)

> The attribute of blame associated with the *nafs* concerns a state which, behind the veils of 'He brings forth [created being, in order to] return' and the reality of 'Having originated with God, one returns to Him' is the awareness of that which is known as Islam. The *Shari'at* becomes the point of focus whereby speech, actions, movement and rest, and the satisfaction of pleasure and gratification are conditioned by this awareness and therefore fall within the limits of the Law.
>
> If the veils themselves are strong and dominating, awareness of Islam becomes concealed, resulting in the violation of the religious law through the actions and indulgence of pleasures which cannot be monitored. Because of this, the possessor of *nafs* may chastise himself and, in the process, attempt to abandon lust and indulgence in pleasure. Here, again, when such awareness arises, the *nafs* will appear, only to confront the religious law which

rejects and obstructs the *nafs* from further indulgence in that which lies outside of its limits. Subsequently, the *nafs* becomes obedient and begins to blame itself. This blaming is of three levels, graded according to their relative grossness or subtlety, namely, Islam, faith, and beneficence. (MD 232)

The blaming *nafs* is that of the sinner and of the elect of the sinners. The Name the 'oppressor', from the Koranic passage referring to those "who oppress themselves," (XXXV:32) is given to them, because, although the light of faith is in their heart, outwardly they act as if they are unbelievers. Thus, in this instance, one is an 'oppressor' where oppression is used in the sense of something being displaced from its rightful place.

In another context, the 'oppressor' conceals the light of faith with the oppressive darkness of transgression, while the 'just person' is one who does not do so.

In a further sense, he is an 'oppressor' of himself because he sins more than he worships. (ME 351)

The blaming *nafs* is that which stands between the commanding *nafs* and the *nafs*-at-rest, and comprises two aspects. One, the aspect of Islam, faces the commanding *nafs*. When it focuses in this direction it blames the commanding *nafs* for the abandonment of spiritual practice, and any steps taken towards resisting God. It also blames itself for all devotions that it has previously lost, as well as for one's attraction to the meadows of bestiality and oppression.

The other aspect is that of faith, which faces the *nafs*-at-rest. When the blaming *nafs* focuses on the *nafs*-at-rest, it becomes illuminated with the light thereof, assuming its hue. It chastises itself for the offences it has committed and the obstructions it has placed before itself. Its persistent blaming leads to ultimate realization of the station of serenity. (RB X 243)

The blaming *nafs* is that which has become illuminated by the light of the heart. When remembrance of God becomes established in the *nafs* that commands one to evil, it becomes lit like a lamp in a dark house, at which point it turns to 'blaming', for it notices that the house is full of filth, and dogs, pigs, tigers, panthers, donkeys, cows, elephants, in short, everything that is blameworthy. Having observed these things, it strives to expel the filth and the animals' savage presence from the house, whereupon it is accompanied by remembrance of God and contrition, until the remembrance overwhelms these things and drives them out. (FJ 25)

The blaming *nafs* is a seeker and a seeking *nafs* leads to a full heart. (RQR 75)

The blaming *nafs* is that term used for the *nafs* at the initial stage of the process of returning to God and renouncing of transgression. It chastises one for immersing oneself in the sites of self-destruction. (EK II 43)

The blaming *nafs* is that which is illuminated by the light of the heart to such a degree that it is awakened from the sleep of heedlessness and begins to purify itself. At this point, it wavers between Lordship and created being. If one commits bad acts due to the darkness of one's nature, one can remedy this through the light of Divine awakening and 'blame'. This process leads one from the misdoings of the *nafs* to the seeking of forgiveness at the court of the Compassionate and All-forgiving. (ES 95[1])

In the intermediate stages of the Path, when the domain of one's existence becomes graced by the control of one's heart, the *nafs* becomes bound by the cord of devotion and will comply with the conventions thereof. However, there will remain many rebellious and aggressive characteristics of the persistent *nafs* which will need to be chastised by that which is known as the blaming *nafs*. (MH 84)

The blaming *nafs* has ten characteristics: asceticism, piety, continence, devotion, commitment to prayer, fasting, the Pilgrimage, supererogatory pilgrimage, payment of the religious tax, and spiritual combat. (RSh I 340)

The blaming *nafs* is the same as the intellect.(SS 632)

All told, the blaming *nafs* has both subtle and gross aspects. Although it chastises, it is also capable of both good and bad actions.

The inspired nafs

The inspired *nafs* is that which God inspires to distinguish between the way of right guidance and that of misguidance. The Sufis have derived this term from the Koranic passage: "And God inspired the

---

1. TJ

nafs with awareness of what is wrong for it and what is right for it." (XCI: 8)

Some of the statements made by Sufi masters concerning the inspired *nafs*, are quoted below:

> When the sun of Divine favor rises above the horizon of right guidance, the *nafs* becomes inspired and illuminated by that sun, so that it is able to distinguish between right and wrong. (RB IV 275)

> The inspired *nafs* is so called because God inspires it to do good, whereby whatever good works the devotee performs are done through Divine inspiration. Whatever bad deeds are done spring from the dictates of material nature and take the form of a command to act. This is why it is called the commanding *nafs*, except in those cases where it is affected by Divine inspiration, when it is called inspired. (EK II 43)

> When a light from the sublime human spirit emanates upon the blaming *nafs*, the *nafs* comes to distinguish between right and wrong, according to the Koranic passage, "And He inspires it with awareness of what is wrong for it and what is right for it." (XCI: 8) Exercising ascetic discipline, it avoids what is forbidden and complies with what is obligatory, whence it is known as the inspired *nafs*. (RSh I 347)

> The inspired *nafs* has ten characteristics: reason, wisdom, knowledge, revelation, inspiration, awareness, perfection, grace, beneficence, and generosity. (RSh I 341)

Consequently, the inspired *nafs* avoids all that is evil and tends towards all that is good.

> Know that the inspired *nafs* is one which has been elevated by the ennoblement of God's inspiration, having been granted the rank of being sworn upon by God, as indicated in the Koranic passage, "And [I swear by] the *nafs* and that which perfected it, and inspired it with awareness of what is wrong for it and what is right for it." (XCI: 7 - 8) The inspired *nafs* stands in the second rank in the realm of the spirits. It is also cited in the Koran as that which is the second level, "And amongst them are those who oppress themselves and among them those who are lukewarm." (XXXV: 32)
>
> The expression 'one who takes the middle course' is applied to

one who stands between the two realms; that of the advanced, who stand in the first rank, on the one hand, and that of the oppressors, on the other, who are in the third rank. It represents the *nafs* of the ordinary friends of God and the elect of the believers. It is ennobled by God's inspiration through the aptitude that has come to it, where, in the realm of the spirits, the spirits of the prophets and the elect of God's friends stand between it and the plane of the Might. A reflection of the emanation of Divine Grace that reaches those of the first rank reaches those in the second rank, who receive a portion of that grace and acquire the savor of God's words from behind the veil. When they have become linked to this realm, even though bedeviled with the characteristics of the commanding *nafs*, the savor of God's grace does not disappear from the palate of their souls, and the pleasure of hearing the words, "Am I not your Lord?" (VII: 172), remains in their hearts.

At no station is the *nafs* more vulnerable or in more in danger, than at the station of inspiration, where it has yet to experience total liberation from self, through gaining savor of inspiration and the Unseen. It is ever at risk of falling into the deception of having attained the station of perfection and being lured into the trap of Satan's temptation, of regarding itself with conceit, of susceptibility to flattery, of self-importance, and of self-promotion. If it so falls it becomes the Eblis of the moment and is flung to the ground by the gale of God's curse, like a fully bloomed blossom falling from the tree of God's approval. (ME 359 & 363)

The nafs at rest:

The *nafs*-at-rest: the nafs is said to be at the station of repose when it has found calm and repose through God, when its light has become perfected through the light of the heart, and when it has irrevocably returned to its Lord. The Sufis derive the term 'serene *nafs*' from the Koranic passage, "O *nafs*-at-rest return to your Lord, contenting, contented." (LXXXIX: 27-28)

The following are some of the statements that masters of the Path have made concerning the *nafs* at rest:

> When the sun of God's favor reaches the zenith of the sky of right guidance, and shines upon the earth of the *nafs* with the light of the Lord, it becomes at-rest and ready to be addressed by these words of the Lord, "Return to your Lord, content in His good pleasure." (LXXXIX: 27-28) (RB IV 275)

The *nafs*-at-rest is that upon which tranquility has descended, and which has become illuminated by the light of certitude, peaceful in God, and liberated from distress. (RB X 433)

When the commanding *nafs* is jolted with the shock of overpowering love it is transformed into the *nafs*-at-rest. (AA 99)

When the blaming *nafs* has become purified of defilement and affliction through the aid of remembrance and contrition, it becomes closer to the *nafs* at rest and constantly tries to clean the house of the heart of all impurities. It prepares to adorn it with all praiseworthy things so that the King of love will enter therein. When the King arrives and God is manifested, the *nafs* will be at-rest. (FJ 25)

When the roots of conflict and misgivings are severed from the *nafs* it becomes serene through the release of strife and agitation of the heart, and docile under the influence of Divine decrees, whereby its misgivings are transformed into contentment and it becomes known as the *nafs*-at-rest. (MH 84)

The *nafs*-at-rest is that which is illuminated by the light of the heart to such an extent that it is purged of all blameworthy attributes and becomes characterized by praiseworthy attributes, completely centering its attention on the heart, and accompanying it in its descent to the realm of sanctity while being cleansed of all impurities and assiduous in its devotions. In this way it travels towards God, where because of his detachment from the world, He addresses it saying, "O *nafs* at rest, return to your Lord contenting, contented. Enter among my devotees and enter my heavens."(LXXXIX:27-30) (ES 96)

The *nafs* at rest is said to be within the heart. (SS 632)

The *nafs* at rest possesses ten characteristics: poverty, patience, justice, fairness, contentment, knowledge, realization, certitude, honor, and fidelity. (RSh I 340)

In sum, the *nafs* at rest is that which has attained the level of the heart and gained the capacity to reach that of the spirit.

Interpretation of Dreams of the Wayfarer's Nafs

When the *nafs* of the novice seeker has been inwardly and outwardly cleansed and purified of the defilement of transgression, by the water of repentance and contrition, it finds itself in the imaginal realm, where it enjoys the blessing of outward worship and devotion and engages in remembrance *(dhekr)* whereby it dreams of flourishing mansions, fine buildings, lush meadows, trees abundant with fruit, and plentiful game.

If the wayfarer dreams of a flourishing mansion, it represents the house of his being, which flourishes through abstinence, the renunciation of lustful and corrupt tendencies, and lack of all excess. If the wayfarer dreams of a lush meadow, it represents the earth of his being, that which has become purified and animated by ablution, remembrance and worship.

If the wayfarer dreams of a temperate atmosphere, it represents soundness of body and a balanced constitution on his part. Wheat, barley, rice, millet. peas and the like represent different forms of religion, different sects, doctrines, traditions, and customs of the *shari'at* and the spiritual Path.

Each of these grains, which symbolize a particular state enjoyed by a wayfarer at a given moment, may be identified by the skillful interpreter. Since there is not always an exact correspondence between symbols and states, there is no point in going into any great detail.

The walnut symbolizes the effective result of the exoteric sciences in most cases, the almond that of the esoteric sciences, the pistachio that of the fine sciences of mathematics and music, and the grape that of the daily prayers. Generally speaking, syrup represents the sweetness of devotions, vinegar the rigor thereof, and wine the intoxication and loving-kindness of love. Persian melon symbolizes the effective result of the term, Divine Unity *(tauḥid)*.

The cucumber represents the joy that comes into consciousness due to God's acceptance of one's states, mixed greens the form of self-worship. Watermelon symbolizes the result of remembrance recited in a state of depression or dampening of heat, or prevailing moistness. Apples, pears, quinces, pomegranates, figs, plums, apricots, peaches and mulberries, although not restricted to one meaning, generally represent an attribute of the effective results of glorifying God, praising God, and magnifying God's Name, or of supplicatory prayers, litanies, readings of the Koran or other forms of worship. Roses, aromatic plants and blossoms in general, represent the spirit, the purity of recited remembrance, and devotions that are observed without reluctance or laziness but rather with full enthusiasm.

Fragrant perfumes represent the breezes which bear the aroma of loving-kindness to the noses of the souls of those who long for Divine encounter. At this level, bodily form and recited remembrance gain the fullness of purity and a light appears, which gives off a greenish glow resulting from actions that have been produced by the limbs of a purified outward form. In the realm of the physical elements the color green embraces all the colors, being that which is possessed by the leaves of trees and plants. The green light is the effective result of worship by the physical body at the level of refinement of the *nafs* from Satanic, predatory, bestial and blameworthy traits. As long as the vile *nafs* is beset by Satanic attributes, it is commanding. Once it is rid of predatory traits, it becomes inspired. Finally, once the inspired *nafs* has been refined of bestial characteristics, it becomes at rest, and a blue light, which is the sign of refinement of the *nafs* and of serenity, appears in the imaginal realm.

If the wayfarer dreams of a monster while governed by his commanding *nafs*, this represents all his false and flaccid traits. If he dreams of a snake, it represents the attribute of hypocrisy or that of the most repugnant lust for that which is forbidden. If he dreams of a dragon, it represents attachment to the world or one who seeks things of the world.

If the wayfarer sees quicklime, it represents pretention. If he sees a scorpion, it symbolizes the attribute of miserliness or a miserly person. If he sees a bee, it represents envy; if a tarantula, it stands for excessive miserliness; if a house on fire, it represents oppression; if burning cloths, they stand for depravity; one's own body on fire where one feels the pain, this represents infidelity; if a dark house, it symbolizes inward turbidity due to consumption of something forbidden; if a polluted house, it stands for love of the world, if a house full of horror, it represents corruption of belief.

The difference between the Satanic attributes of the commanding *nafs* and the predatory ones of the blaming *nafs* lies in the fact that the former is evil and enjoins evil; that is, it is both misguided and misguiding while the latter is evil alone, without enjoining evil, misguided but not misguiding.

While the commanding *nafs* is in the process if being converted into the blaming one, dreams are seen of towering mountains and parched plains, as well as predatory animals of various kinds, If the wayfarer dreams of himself as a panther this represents the attribute of arrogance, if he dreams of the panther itself it represents an arrogant person. If he dreams of himself as a goat it symbolizes rage or cowardice or rashness while if he dreams of the goat itself it represents a cowardly person who makes a boastful display of being brave.

If the wayfarer sees a bear, it represents audacity in pursuit of depravity and cardinal sins or a corrupt person shamelessly indulging in what is forbidden. If he sees a pig, it symbolizes spinelessness and irresponsibility or licentiousness, or apostasy or a person possessing any of these characteristics.

If the wayfarer sees a fat she-donkey, it symbolizes blind imitation of a person in superficial outward movements, not in inward worship. If he sees a fox it represents deception or a deceiving person. If he sees a hare it stands for trickery or a tricky person. If he sees a jackal it symbolizes obstinacy or slander or gossip or thievery or meanness. If he sees a hyena, it represents hidden treachery or falsehood or calumny or delusion or similar traits, or a person possessing any of these.

If the wayfarer sees a wolf, it represents greed or abandonment of the Path or a greedy person or one who abandons the Path or a thief. If he sees a dog, it symbolizes anger or lust for what is forbidden or one who is tyrannical or one who is depraved or one who seeks temporal pleasure. Now, a bitch represents adulterous lust or depravity or one who is adulterously depraved. If one sees a rat, it represents covetousness in the amassing of property or a covetous possessor of property. If he sees a louse, it symbolizes sadness, and if a flea, it represents grief. If he sees a bedbug, it stands for defamation and if a fly, it symbolizes complaint. If he sees a spider it represents hypocrisy.

If he sees a tortoise, it represents ambition with respect to something worldly. If he sees a porcupine, it symbolizes irascibility or anger or jealousy or conceit or even boldness or a bold person. If he sees a tiger it represents courage or triumph or a high rank.

Other predatory animals and insects are symbolic forms of blameworthy traits of character and attributes of meanness. The most extreme blameworthy attributes are represented by fearsome predatory animals and poisonous insects. while the most extreme attributes of meanness are symbolized by weaker predatory animals and non-poisonous insects.

While the blaming *nafs* is in the course of being transmuted into the inspired *nafs* topographical features appear, such as hills and valleys with animals of various kinds grazing there.

If the wayfarer sees a donkey it symbolizes sexual lust, infirmity or idiocy or a person who possesses any of these traits. If he sees a cow, it represents gluttony. If it is an old cow, it means that one has gormandized a great deal. If it is a calf, it represents appetite and obsession with anticipation of eating. If the cow is thin it represents penury. If the cow is very fat it represents over consumption. If there are many cattle, preoccupation with ordinary sustenance or a varied diet.

If the wayfarer sees a mountain-goat it symbolizes fear of the attributes of perfection and avoidance and fear of perfected ones. If he sees a large horn or many horns it represents pride and ambition. If he sees a goat it represents hypocrisy or deceit or a hypocritical or deceitful person. Other domesticated or wild beasts are symbolic forms of kindred or similar characteristics.

While the inspired *nafs* in the course of being transmuted into the one at rest, flat plains appear, lying fallow for cultivation. Also in accordance with the Prophetic dictum, "Die before you die," one experiences death, being washed as a corpse and wrapped in a shroud, having the prayer for the dead recited over one, and being interred. Then, in accordance with the dictum "When one dies and then is resurrected one has experienced the resurrection." one undergoes the lesser resurrection, which is the resurrection of the *nafs*, occurring as a result of voluntary death involving liberation from Satanic, predatory and bestial attributes.

In the early stages of this transformation one sees certain domesticated beasts which are closer to man in their roles, such as horses, camels, sheep and the like. If the wayfarer sees a horse it symbolizes worship and daily prayers *(namāz)*. Mounting the horse symbolizes the performing of obligatory prayers. Mounting the camel represents the performance of the customary prayers in daily practice, and mounting a well-behaved donkey stands for the performance of supererogatory spiritual practices.

Sometimes soldiers and men at arms, and sometimes worshippers and men of peace are represented in the form of the horses which may also symbolize good fortune and the attainment of one's object of desire. If the wayfarer sees an elephant it represents tolerance and endurance or vicegerancy. If he sees a camel it represents Islam. If the camel is carrying a load, this represents nourishment of Islam. If camels are seen in a caravan, this symbolizes the Prophetic custom *(sonnat)* and the Islamic community. If the camel is drunk, it represents love or yearning or ecstasy or recovery of a lost high state, or a lover, yearner, or drunkard.

If the wayfarer sees a sheep, it also symbolizes Islam or a believer. If he sees a mountain-goat which has been broken and domesticated, it represents obedience and zealous devotion or an attracted person who has become a wayfarer.

In the case of vision of birds at any given stage of the heart or any given station, since birds represent the outward form of aspiration *(hemmat)*, and aspiration, whether high or low is involved at all levels, we shall treat birds in the same fashion as the other animals discussed.

Domesticated fowl represents aspiration confined to low things and obsession with sustenance. A rooster stands for aspiration confined to objects of lust and obsession with sex. The sparrow symbolizes aspiration confined to members of the opposite sex who are close to one and obsession with stimulating lust. The pigeon stands for aspiration confined to members of the opposite sex who are distant from one or sending of heavenly emissaries or remembrance *(dhekr)* in the heart. The raven symbolizes aspiration confined to things of the world. The crow represents aspiration confined to miserly concerns in the world. The dove stands for aspiration confined to equivocation in one's thoughts of worldly things. The vulture symbolizes aspiration confined to property and status in the world. The duck represents aspiration confined to cleanliness of dress and performance of ablution. The goose stands for aspiration confined to cleanliness of the body; and the remaining water fowl symbolize aspiration confined to cleansing of the *nafs* from forbidden things or cleansing the heart from distraction and obsession with poetic diversion or with matters involving the cleansing of one's adherence to Unity from the pollution of multiplicity of attachment.

Fish are symbolic of adherence to Divine Unity *(tauḥid)* mixed with gnosis. The bat represents aspiration confined to dogmatic imitation and obsession with formalistic doctrine and distance from the realities of the realized ones. The hoot owl stands for aspiration confined to the world and distance from the friends of God *(wali)* and the associates of the hereafter and obsession with destruction. The partridge symbolizes aspiration confined to daily sustenance and obsession with lawful diet. The quail represents aspiration confined to cunning in obtaining one's daily bread.

The hoopoe stands for aspiration confined to the sending of

divine emissaries and spiritual mission and seeking nearness to kings, whether worldly or spiritual, as well as resolution of dissention. The starling symbolizes aspiration confined to eloquence and instruction and study of the sciences and spiritual knowledge. The parrot represents the establishment of Divine knowledge and the instruction and study of the sciences of the path and of Reality. The crane stands for aspiration confined to the acquisition of lawful food and commerce and hospitality and consumption. The barn-owl symbolizes aspiration confined to remembrance *(dhekr)* and nightly vigil and seclusion. The finch represents aspiration confined to matters which are difficult beyond endurance. The stork stands for aspiration confined to the acquisition of property, and the kite symbolizes aspiration confined to the seeking of the world and unlawful property. The chicken represents aspiration confined to the world and unlawful property as well, while the cock-pheasant stands for aspiration confined to lawful property.

The swallow symbolizes aspiration confined to journeys to distant places and the Pilgrimage *(ḥajj)*. The ostrich represents aspiration confined to the protection of oneself from enemies and mismanagement. The heron stands for aspiration confined to blind imitation and distance from adherence to Divine unity. The nightingale symbolizes aspiration confined to love, audition *(samāʿ)* and music, while the ring dove represents aspiration confined to worship and purification and remembrance in the heart. The wood pigeon stands for aspiration confined to contentment *(qanāʿat)* and habituation and diligence in remembrance and worship. The turtle-dove symbolizes aspiration confined to remembrance at a different spiritual level of the heart and purity of consciousness. The hawk represents aspiration confined to higher spiritual things and those who respond to the appeal to God. The falcon stands for aspiration confined to matters of the Path and guidance of the wayfarers. The kestrel symbolizes aspiration confined to matters of the religious law and instruction of the etiquette thereof. The sparrow-hawk stands for aspiration confined to the observance of Islam. The eagle symbolizes aspiration confined to matters of the realm of sovereignty *(molk)*. The royal eagle represents aspiration confined to matters pertaining to the leadership of a community. The *homā* stands for aspiration confined to ascetic discipline, or the arcane or innermost consciousness *(khafi)* level of heart consciousness, or matters pertaining to the realm of power *(jabarut)*. The simorg symbolizes aspiration confined to theophanies of the divine Essence and annihilation in God and attainment of the realm of Divinity *(lāhut)* and the station of nearness to God. The remaining birds are symbolic in like fashion.

At the level of the *nafs* at rest, certain plants and minerals may be seen, such as cabbage, turnip, celery, beet-root, garlic, onion and the lik;, that is any plant the roots of which are commonly eaten, being considered especially nourishing. When seen cooked, they symbolize the *nafs* at rest. If they are seen raw, this could represent any of the other *nafs*. For example, if the wayfarer sees a poisonous plant, root or branch, it stands for speech and outward actions which he produces, resulting in the destruction of a faithful one. This sort of plant is a symbol for the commanding *nafs*.

If he sees a radish, this represents contempt and abuse arising from the blaming *nafs*. If he sees raw onion or garlic, this symbolizes vileness and caviling and abomination and vilification. Both onion and garlic represent attributes arising from the blaming *nafs*. If he sees cooked onion or garlic, this represents dissuasion from what is forbidden and prevention of foul utterance. If he sees raw cabbage, it stands for sycophancy and leniency. If he sees cooked cabbage, it symbolizes kindness. If he sees raw turnips, it represents weakness and abasement. If he sees cooked turnips, it stands for humility. If he sees raw celery, it symbolizes obstinacy or virility. If he sees cooked celery, it represents compliance and amiability or physical strength. If he sees raw beets, it signifies harsh words, and if cooked then gentle ones. The four proceeding — beet-root, turnip, cabbage and celery — in a raw state represent attributes of the inspired *nafs*, while in a cooked one they stand for attributes of the *nafs* at rest.

At this level of the *nafs* at rest, certain minerals are seen, such as lime, calcium, alum, salt, petroleum, copper, lead, tin, sulphur, arsenic, sal-ammoniac, tutty and the like. Quicklime symbolizes harshness, while slaked lime stands for assiduousness and persistence in remembrance. Crude calcium signifies procrastination and lack of achievement, while calcium which has been treated, pulverized, sifted and prepared as plaster symbolizes denial of the individual consciousness and affirmation of eternity and breaking of the *nafs* and inward purity. Alum represents cheating and malice and envy and rancor. Salt symbolizes courtesy and refinement and training and humility and meekness and submissiveness and manliness and companionship. Petroleum represents figurative love. Copper stands for aptitude for the Path and the Sufi doctrine. The smelting of copper to extract it from the ore symbolizes the refinement of the *nafs* from turbidites of conventions and habits. Lead represents torpor and leniency, while smelted lead stands for acceptance of advice. Tin symbolizes pliancy and sycophancy and flattery, while smelted tin represents trainability.

The wayfarer's progress at the spiritual level of the *nafs* is downwards. This is to say at first, the commanding *nafs* is governed by a fiery nature. When it descends from this fieriness to become the blaming *nafs*, it becomes governed by airiness. Once it has descended from airiness and becomes the inspired *nafs*, it becomes governed by wateriness. Once it has descended from this watery nature and becomes the *nafs*-at-rest, it becomes governed by earthiness, gaining stability, whereupon it becomes characterized by humility, dignity, meekness and submissiveness. When the Satanic, predatory and bestial characteristics have been transmuted into human ones, one comes to enjoy frequent dreams of human beings, such as believers, ascetics, doers of good works, righteous people, peacemakers, pure people, worshippers and possessors of *nafs*-at-rest. (RN 151)

HEARTS

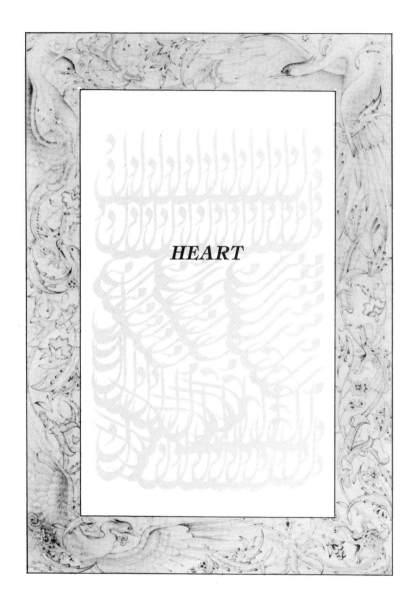

HEART

Become a person of the heart
—or at least the devotee of one;
Or else, you will remain
like a donkey stuck in the mud.

If one has no heart,
one can gain no benefit;
In wretchedness, one
will be famous in the world.
SGR 144

When the *nafs* has reached the ultimate degree of perfection, it passes on to the level of the heart.

In fact, the *nafs* at rest is the very heart, referred to by the philosophers as the rational *nafs* (*nafs-e nāṭeqa*). Most people, however, are at the psychological levels of material nature (*tab*‘) and of the *nafs*, and have no heart.

The heart is a city between the domain of Unity (spirit, *ruh*) and the land of multiplicity *(nafs)*. If the heart snaps the cord linking it with the *nafs*, it falls under the sway of the spirit; that is to say, it becomes *heart* in the true sense of the word, polished clean of the corrosion of multiplicity. On the other hand, if the heart becomes dominated by the *nafs*, it becomes darkened by the tarnish of the *nafs'* multiplicity, taking on its hue.

The spirit is the source of all good, and the *nafs* of all evil. Love constitutes the army of the spirit, and the passions that of the *nafs*.

The spirit represents success through God, while the *nafs* represents failure through God. The heart lies between these two rulers, and the victor of the two rulers conquers the heart.

When love calls
the heart to it,
The heart flees
from all creation.

Rumi

The heart is the site of all knowledge and perfections of the spirit and the site of the appearance of the revelations of Divine Manifestations through different levels of the Essence. It is this aspect that gives it its Arabic name *qalb* (revolution), indicating its mediate position between the *nafs* and the spirit. It constitutes a bridge between the two, manifesting the perfections of the two levels that flank it, deriving grace from the spirit and conveying it to the *nafs*.

The world-displaying Cup
is the heart of the Perfect Man;
The mirror reflecting God
is, in fact, the very heart.

SGR 3

The clay of Adam was made
malleable by the dew of love;
As a result, a hundred calamities
and turmoils appeared in the world.

The lancet of love
pricked the vein of the spirit.
A drop dripped down,
and its name became heart.

Majdo'd-Din Baghdādi

In his commentary on the *Foṣuṣ al-ḥekam*, Jāmi writes:

"The heart is the reality that encompasses both the realities of corporeality and the faculties of the physical constitution on the one hand, and the realities of spirituality and the characteristics of the *nafs*, on the other."

In Sufi terminology, the heart represents an incorporeal luminous substance situated between the spirit and the *nafs*, a substance through which humanity is realized. The philosophers call this substance the rational *nafs*, maintaining that it is mounted upon the animal *nafs*. (KF 1170)

In this domain,
the king is the heart;
In the way of the lote-tree,[1]
the threshold is the heart.

The body is nothing,
one's essence is the heart;
The dweller "between the two fingers"[2]
of God is the Heart.

It is capable of the role
of either religion or infidelity;
It can churn up kindness or malice,
either one equally.

You have heard the tale of Jamshid's cup[3]
recounted often enough,
And in that tale you have heard full well
the more or less of things.

Be well aware that Jamshid's cup
is your heart,
That your heart constitutes the seat of both
joy and sorrow.

If you make an appeal
to see the world,
You'll be able to see
all things therein.

M140

The rosebush of the soul
was planted in hope
of the budding
of the rose of the heart.

When that rosebush
then produced
The freshly budding
rose of the heart,

1. The lote-tree is the symbolic marker of the frontier between individual consciousness and Divine Union (Koran LIII:14).
2. Reference to the Prophetic Tradition: "The heart of the believer is held between two fingers of the merciful; He turns it about as He wills." See the author's *Traditions of the Prophet* vol. II pp. 12-13.
3. The Persian equivalent of the crystal ball, bestowed upon the legendary founder of the Iranian ethos, Shāh Jamshid.

Enfolded in that bud were found
the petals of whatever
May be found in creation,
whether particular or universal.

The beauty of the beauteous
is the sign of His grace;
The realm of space and time
is the book of His multiplicity

The universe and whatever lies therein,
And whatever is called wisdom
that makes up His world

Is lost in the vastness
of the realm of the heart,
All but a drop
in the heart, the Red Sea.

How can one measure
That which contains God?

The heart that lies
within the veil of the body
Is subject to life and death.

The manifestation of divine mysteries
and the reflection of divine lights
Lie not in the physical heart
but in the true heart.

If the heart were but a thing of clay,
there would be no distinction
Between this heart and that of a donkey.

How long will you boast
of this thing of clay?
The donkey also profits
from this instrument.

Whoever, like a donkey,
gives value to this instrument,
Exchanges a precious pearl
for a clay bead.

You must submit
to an ocean-hearted one
If you wish to find the heart
that is such a pearl.
You must pitch your tent

beside the master,
If you want to gain
a heart from him.

Your heart is the egg
of a fine bird:
There is no trace of movement,
of flight therein.

To animate it,
to make it fly,
Give it to the master
who will make it hatch.

HAu 388

Why The Spiritual Heart Is Called Heart

The heart with which the Sufis are concerned is not the physical organ of that name. The physical heart is a piece of flesh located on the left side of the body under the breastbone. The reason for using the term heart to represent the spiritual heart is due to its relationship with the physical heart.

The physical heart is in a constant state of alteration, regulating the changes between arterial or subtle blood and venal or gross blood. The spiritual heart is also in a constant state of alteration, here rotating back and forth between the subtle influences of the spirit and the gross influences of the *nafs*. This is where the heart derives its Arabic name, *qalb*, from the root *q-l-b*, meaning to revolve or turn over.

The physical heart sends blood to the arteries and receives the gross blood of the veins; it is essential to the processes of purifying the human body. Likewise, the spiritual heart receives the gross traits of the *nafs* and purifies them with the help of the spirit, converting them into spiritual traits of character, to foster the soundness of a person's psyche. Actually, the heart is a median between the subtle realities of the psyche and the gross characteristics of the *nafs*.

Just as the corporeal life of each person is connected to the physical heart, such that if the heart is injured the person becomes ill, or if it stops working the person dies, so the spiritual life of each individual is linked to the spiritual heart, such that if this heart becomes afflicted by characteristics of the *nafs*, the person becomes ill-natured, and if this heart becomes completely overpowered by the *nafs*, dying so to speak, the spiritual life of the individual will cease.

The physical heart is a field for the interplay between the veins that bring gross blood, and the arteries that carry subtle blood enriched with oxygen, which becomes the subtle air of the lungs, the breath. The spiritual heart is likewise, a field for the interplay between the gross forces of the *nafs* and the subtle forces of the spirit, the spiritual breath.

The physical heart is called such because of its relatively central location in the body. By the same token, the spiritual heart is called thus because in the process of the perfection of the individual's psyche it plays a role at the midpoint between the *nafs* and the spirit.

Just as the physical heart maintains the continued functioning of the body through its perpetual and spontaneous action, the spiritual heart automatically regulates the temperament and psychological actions. The physical heart governs the physical body, while the spiritual heart governs the psyche.

> The spiritual heart is called *qalb* because of its turning through the stages of states in the process of advancement towards perfection. Given that states are divinely bestowed and that things which are bestowed by God are infinite in number, the turning and progress that one makes on the way to perfection, with all the permutations of the pre-eternal Beauty and Majesty, are infinitely varied. (MH 97)

> The heart is called *qalb* because it is the site of the manifestation of different aspects of God, revealing a different aspect at every moment, turning (*monqaleb*) from Attribute to Attribute. It moves also between that aspect which constitutes an interface with God and that aspect which serves as an interface with the creation. That is, it receives grace from God and passes it on to the creation. (SGR 4)

The heart is a site
of Divine Manifestation:
How could one call
the devil's house a heart?

Go and throw
that physical thing
you call a heart
to the dogs!

The true heart is such
that even in a moment of catastrophe
You find absolutely nothing
therein but God.

Nuro'd- Din Esfārāyini[1]

Not Everyone Has a Heart.

It is important to note that amongst all created things only human beings may possess a spiritual heart.

However, from the point of view of the progress of the psyche, the majority of people are no more advanced than the level of material nature (*ṭab'*) or the *nafs*. Only a few people have reached that level of the heart where it can properly be said that they have a heart.

According to the Koran: "Lo, therein verily is a reminder for him who hath a heart." (L: 37)

O heart, sit with someone
who knows the heart;
Go under the tree
which has fresh blossoms.
Rumi

The Living Heart and the Dead Heart

The heart is a battleground between the armies of the spirit or spiritual characteristics and a praiseworthy temperament, on the one hand, and those of the *nafs* or the characteristics of the *nafs* and a blameworthy temperament, on the other. If the field of the heart falls under the sway of the *nafs* and its attributes, the heart becomes dead, whereas if the space of the heart becomes filled with spiritual and human attributes, the heart becomes alive, and one who possesses such a heart is called a *sāheb-del* (heart-possessor) and is known as a person of heart (*ahl-e del*).

Most people's hearts are in a state of flux between dead-heartedness and live-heartedness, though most tend towards the former, while only a limited number tend towards the latter.

> When someone asked Jonaid when the heart is truly content, he replied, "When it is truly a heart."(TA 428)

Do not Confuse the Heart and the Nafs!

Ordinary people tend to confuse the heart with the *nafs*. When someone says "It is my heart's desire that...", it is not the heart that is desiring; the desire comes from the *nafs*. When one says, "This appeals" or "does not appeal to my heart," it is not the heart but the

---

1. See KAM 137.

nafs which accepts or rejects that thing; the heart is above acceptance or rejection.

When one says, "It strikes my heart that something is going to happen" it indicates that the heart is influenced by the *nafs*. The perfect heart sees both pre-eternity and post-eternity; it has no need for prediction or miraculous powers.

The heart of a heart possessor has no desire. This is indicated in the story of the dervish who was asked what his heart desired. He replied, "That my heart should have no desire." In the invocation (*qonut*) of his daily prayers (*namāz*), Bāyazid would exclaim, "Lord, You know what I want!" It is of such a heart that the Prophet said, "The heart of the believer is held between two fingers of the merciful; He turns it about as He wills."[1]

Self-consciousness, Unconsciousness, and Heart -Consciousness

People may be classified into three categories with respect to material nature *(ṭab')*, *nafs* and heart:

The first category is that of the unconscious, who live at the psychological level of material nature and are concerned solely with eating and sleeping and sex. This is the type referred to as the primitive or savage human.

The second category is that of the self-conscious, those who live at the psychological level of the *nafs* and enjoy all the characteristics as described above to which are added ambition, selfishness and status-seeking, all of which stem from self-love and egocentricity. This is the type referred to as a civilized person.

The third category is that of the heart-conscious, those who are at the psychological level of the heart, having become liberated from the ego. They are the elect, the possessors of heart, who have passed from intellectual awareness to vision of the realities of things as they truly are.

Historically speaking, one may equate these categories to successive ages of mankind. In this respect, the present era may be viewed as one of self-consciousness. It may take centuries for man to enter the age of heart-consciousness and build the promised paradise in this world. Although such a notion is no more than a cherished hope, it is worth consideration bearing in mind the constant drive of man's psychic advance towards perfection.

1. *Traditions*, Vol. II, pp. 12-13.

The Dead Heart

When Ḥasan Baṣri was asked why his words did not awaken the sleeping hearts of his disciples, he replied, "If only they were merely asleep, for what is asleep will wake up when shaken, but your hearts are dead! However much one shakes them, they will not wake up!" (TA 33)

Mālek Dinār said, "I asked Ḥasan what the consequences of involvement with the world would be, and he replied, 'The death of the heart.' Then I asked what 'death of the heart' was, and he answered, 'Love of the world.'" (TA 37)

Kharaqāni said, "Any heart that contains anything other than God—even if it is all worship—is a dead heart." (TA 697)

The Awakened Heart

Rābe'a said, "O children of Adam, there are no stages between the eye and God, no access to Him by the tongue; the ear of listeners strains in vain, and the hands and feet are but the rudder of bewilderment. This work is for the heart alone. Strive to acquire a heart that's awake, for when the heart awakens, one needs no beloved, for the awakened heart is one that is lost in God, and whoever is so lost needs no beloved. This is annihilation in God." (TA 81)

The Contraction and Expansion of the Heart

Bāyazid said, "The contraction of the heart occurs with the expansion of the *nafs*, and the other way around." (TA 196)

The Corruption of the Heart

Foḍhail 'Eyāḍh said, "There are two characteristics which corrupt the heart: sleeping too much and over-eating." (TA 99)

The Lack of Presence of Heart

Ebrāhim Adham said, "The door is closed to the heart that is not present in the following three instances: when reading the Koran, when engaged in remembrance (*dhekr*), and when saying one's prayers (*namaz*)." (TA 112)

The Ailing Heart

Dho'n-Nun Meṣri said, "There are four symptoms of an ailing heart: not finding sweetness in one's worship, not fearing God, not heeding admonition, and not understanding the knowledge that is taught to one." (TA 152)

The Gnosis of the Unity of Being Particular to the Heart

Knowledge of the 'Unity of Being' (*waḥdat-e wojud*) belongs to the heart, and one who is not a possessor of heart cannot realize the true meaning of this with certitude; such a one can only mimic understanding thereof through the testimony of gnostics.

The gnostic's heart
knows Being;
It enjoys vision
of absolute Being.

GR 28

The Heart as Having a Spiritual Quality

Manṣur ebn 'Ammār said, "The hearts of the devoted are completely spiritual. If the world enters such a heart, the spirit, which had graced it, becomes veiled." (TA408)

The Heart of the Friend of God as the Site of God's Mystery

Jonaid said, "The heart of the friend of God is the site of God's mystery, and God does not place His Mysteries in the heart of one who loves the world." (TA 438)

Preservation of the Heart

Preservation of the heart is of two kinds: if the heart is preserved through Reality, it becomes preserving, while if it is preserved by God, it is said to be preserved. Thus, the preserving heart is one which is conscious of Reality, while the preserved heart is protected from heedlessness. (TKQ 517)

The Heart as Leading the Way

Abu Bakr Wāseṭi said, "All the heavens have the tongue of praise and glorification, but it is the heart that is necessary, for it is a spiritual reality that exists solely in humankind. It is the heart that closes the door of lust and desire, of acquisitiveness and self-will; it is your leader and guide. It must be the tongue of the heart that calls you, not the vocal tongue. One must be mute with the tongue and speak through the heart, rather than the other way around. (TA 737)

Advisor, it is absurd
to tell my heart to let Him go!
I obey my heart
My heart does not obey me.

Ḥelāli Joghtā'i

The Admonisher of the Heart

Abu 'Ali Rudbāri said, "Everything has an admonisher, and that of the heart is shame." (TA 757)

The Liberated State of the Heart

Shebli said, "Service is the liberated state of the heart." (TA 634)

The Spiritual Realities of the Heart

Abo'l-Ḥasan Kharaqāni said: "The heart has three spiritual realities: annihilation, blessing and subsistence. Its state of annihilation provides a haven at the stage of spiritual poverty, that of blessing a haven at the stage of self-sufficiency through God, and that of subsistence a haven for God Himself. (TA 708)

Subsistence of Hearts is Through God

Abu Bakr Wāseṭi said, "The life and subsistence of the heart is through God; moreover, it is in absence from God in God. As long as you see yourself as belonging to God, then you are a dualist. The annihilation of annihilation is achieved through annihilation." (TA 744)

The Heart as a Wave of the Sea

Abo'l-Ḥasan Kharaqāni said, "One must see one's heart as a wave, a wave from the midst of which fire springs, consuming the body. The tree of fidelity sprouts up amidst what is consumed, bearing in turn the fruit of abiding subsistence in God. When one eats this fruit, its juice soaks down into the heart, penetrating it, annihilating one in the unity thereof." (TA 691)

The Gnostic's Heart is like a Lamp

Bāyazid said, "The gnostic's heart is like a lamp in a candelabrum made of unblemished mirror work, such that its radiance illuminates the entire angelic realm (*malakut*). What then does it have to fear from darkness?" (TA 197)

The Heart as Being Constantly in a State of Revolution

The heart is called *qalb* (that which turns or revolves) in Arabic, because it is constantly in a state of turning or revolution, passing from state to state. With every revolution it acquires new knowledge, each piece of knowledge drawing it on to a new reality, each reality providing a way to gnosis of God. (TKQ 391)

At every moment the heart
follows another doctrine,
Follows another way,
another convention and religion.
Maghrebi

The Absence of Desire for Created Being in the Heart

When Bāyazid Basṭāmi was asked to explain the heart, he said, "The heart is that which contains not the slightest particle of desire for created being." (KAM VIII 232)

The sanctuary of the heart is no place
for association with other things;
When the devil is expelled therefrom
the angels settle in.
Ḥāfeẓ

Cure for the Heart

Ebrāhim Khawwāṣ said, "There are five cures for the heart: reading and contemplating the Koran, keeping one's stomach empty, keeping the night vigil in supplication until dawn, and associating with the virtuous." (TA 608)

The Heart in the Hands of the Beloved

When Kharaqāni was asked about the state of his heart, he replied, "For forty years my heart has been cut off from me." (TA 697)

The Veil of the Heart

Ebrāhim Adham said, "Three veils must be removed from the heart of the gnostic for the gate of success to be opened to him.

If all that exists in the two worlds were bestowed upon one, one would not rejoice, because this would mean rejoicing in created being, indicating that one is still covetous, and the covetous person is barred from success.

If one possessed all that exists in the two worlds and had it taken away, one would not grieve at the loss for this would be a sign of miserliness, and the miserly person is punished.

If one were praised or blamed, one would not be deceived by this, for this would indicate that one is of low aspiration, and a person of low aspiration is veiled. One must be of high aspiration." (TA 112)

The Consigning of the Gnostc's Heart to God

Rābe'a said, "The gnostic is one who desires a heart from God. When God gives him one, he returns it immediately to be preserved in God's grasp and veiled from the creation in the Unseen." (TA 81)

I stopped caring about
being sound and healthy
When this heart placed the reins
in the palm of Your hand.

Ḥāfeẓ

The Sufi's Heart as the Home and Site of Love

If the heart comes to terms
with the sorrow of love,
It will come mounted
on the steed of desire.
If there were no heart,
where would love build a home?
If there were no love,
what function would the heart have?

Sa'do'd-Din Ḥamuya

Purity of the Heart

Abo'l-Khair Aqṭa' said: "The heart can be purified only through correct intention towards God, and the body can be purified only through service to the Friends of God (*wali*)."

"In God's creation there is a fundamental difference between one kind of heart and another. One serves as the site of faith, the indication of which is kindness to all Moslems, striving in the service of them, and aiding them in what is right for them. The other kind of heart serves as the site of hypocrisy, the indication of which is rancor, deception and envy." (TA 549)

Infidelity of the Heart

Infidelity of the heart occurs in three instances:

During meditation (*morāqaba*) where one's attention is distracted from God's existence, this distraction making one an infidel.

In the course of communication [with God], where if one appeals to God for something other than God, or speaks of one's self, one is an infidel.

In the time of self-examination (*moḥāsaba*), where in the course of correcting one's inner consciousness (*serr*), one becomes veiled from lights, because of concern with things other than God. In so doing one enumerates God's acts before God, and by limiting God's acts, he becomes an infidel. If one fails to see the agent, one is an infidel. (RQR 84)

Breadth of the Heart

When a person's heart becomes the site of the manifestation of the plane of Divinity, it becomes a mirror for the limitless Divine aspects to the extent of its capacity and aptitude. Of all the levels of existence, only the heart of the Perfect Man has the breadth to contain the Divine Being, as indicated in the Prophetic tradition: "Neither My heavens nor My earth can contain Me. Yet the heart of My believing devotee contains Me."[1]

The heart is the site of the manifestation of the Name, the Just (*al-'Adl*), and is involved in maintaining the equilibrium of the body, as well as the *nafs*, its faculties, and the spirit. Of all the

1. *Traditions,* vol. I, p. 25.

levels of existence only the heart observes the outward and inward decrees, for it constitutes the form of the Oneness of Concentration (*aḥadiyat-e jam'*) between the outer and the inner. For this reason, it has become the site of the manifestation of all the Divine aspects. Furthermore, man's comprehensiveness and perfection exist through this heart.

Know, in fact, that the heart
is the Cup of Jamshid;
Everything great or small
is displayed therein.
The heart is the mirror of the Essence
of the Majestic One;
God's beauty
shows in the pure one's heart.
God cannot fit
in the heavens and the earth;
Know that He fits
in the believer's heart alone.
No one has seen the limit
of the dominions of the heart;
The heart serves as a sign
of God's Allembracingness.
The heart is the site of the manifestation
of God's aspects;
It manifests the aspects of God
"as they are."[1]

By virtue of its position as a bridge between the outer and the inner, the heart represents an amalgamation of opposites, where, as Shabestari says in the *Golshan-e rāz:*

Both worlds are brought
together therein;
Sometimes it becomes
Eblis, sometimes Adam.

Since the human heart is the site of the manifestation of the Divine Concentration, the realities of all outward and inward levels, namely, the two worlds, are equally contained therein. All the opposing Divine Names, whether of Majesty or Beauty, are manifest according to the heart's capacity, and every instant it shows a different manifestation or aspect under the varying con-

1. Reference to the Prophetic Tradition "O Lord, show me things as they are." *Traditions*, vol. I, p 32.

trol of these Names. At one moment, it may become Eblis under the domination of the Majestic Names, for Eblis is a manifestation particular to these names; at another time it may become Adam, influenced by the Beautiful Names, since in Adam the Beautiful Attributes predominate and the Majestic Names are suppressed. Consequently, the heart's state does not remain constant, so that at every moment it displays a different world and at every instant a different attitude and aspect.

There are a hundred idol-temples
in every corner of the heart,
On every side a hundred Ka'bas,
a hundred sites of worship.
Sometimes it hovers
in the upper world;
Sometimes its station
is the lower one.
Sometimes it is independent,
sometimes under influence;
Sometimes it is in Union,
sometimes separated.
Sometimes it becomes an angel,
sometimes a malignant devil;
Sometimes it is an intellect
sometimes entirely nafs.

SGR 118

The world-displaying cup
is the heart of the Perfect Man;
The mirror reflecting God
is in fact this very heart.

The heart is the treasury
in which God's mysteries are stored;
Seek the purpose of both the worlds
through the heart, for that is
the point of it.

SGR 3

Breadth of the heart is of three kinds:

Breadth of knowledge, which is gnosis of God, where there is nothing in existence which knows the effects of God like the heart; for every being knows its Lord in one form or another, but only the heart knows Him completely.

Breadth of vision, which involves the revelation through which the heart is made aware of the virtues of God's Beauty. The heart experiences God's Names and Attributes through vision. This is the situation of the gnostic.

Breadth of vicegerency, involves the realization of God's Names and Attributes, until the heart experiences its essence as God's Essence, and the devoted one's self identity becomes God's Self-identity (*howiyat*). As God's vicegerent, one wields control in the world. This is the situation of the realised ones. (KF 1171)

The lover has a heart that transcends determination (*ta'ayyon*), being the ground on which the cupolas of the Might are erected as well as the confluence of the seas of the Unseen and the visible. The aspiration of this heart is so great that:

If it sips a thousand seas
of wine by the cupful,
Its aspiration would be
to drink still more wine.

Accordingly, the heart has such a breadth that the entire universe could not accommodate it; the whole universe would disappear as an infinitesimal speck in its grasp. It pitches the pavilion of singularity (*fardāniyat*) in the courtyard of uniqueness (*waḥdaniyat*), building the palace of Divine kingship and performing its operations there, loosening and tightening, contracting and expanding, fluctuating and stabilizing.

When it contracts;
the heart hides what it has launched;
And when it expands
it returns what it has hidden
I am astounded that the Idol whose beauty
is such that it cannot fit into the world,
Can take up permanent
residence in my tiny heart.

Speaking of the breadth of his own heart, Bāyazid said, "If the Throne and all that it contains were to be placed in a corner of the gnostic's heart, the gnostic would not be aware of it."

Since Bāyazid's heart was thus, he saw everything as the Eternal, hence his ecstatic exclamation: 'Glory be to me!'"

Jonaid said, "When the transitory joins the Eternal, nothing of it remains." (Lm 36)

The Sight and Insight of the Heart

Whenever the heart becomes purified of the effects of the *nafs* and its veiling, it sees the angelic realm (*malakut*), and the degrees of the Unseen and the mysteries of its domains are revealed to him. As the Prophet stated, "If devils were not circulating in people's hearts, they would see the celestial angelic realm." This is only the beginning of the heart's vision. As it ascends higher, the lights of God's Attributes become revealed to it; this is the witnessing (*moshāhada*) of the Attributes. When 'Ali ebn Abi Taleb was asked if he saw God, he replied, "How could I worship someone I have not seen? Eyes cannot see him through direct revelation [in the world], but the heart sees Him through the realities of faith."

According to the Koran, "The heart does not lie in what it sees." (LIII:11) Masters have said that the heart's vision is of that which is hidden behind the veils of the Unseen through the lights of certitude or the realities of faith.

The Prophet stated, "Worship God as if you see Him; for even if you do not see Him, He sees you."

The gnostic said, "The heart's vision represents its encounter with God's theophany during the course of the wayfarer's shedding of all conventions." (MA 125)

The eye of the heart is focused on the effects of the Unseen with certitude and the reality of faith. The reality of this vision arises from the encounter between the eye of the spirit and the beauty of the realm of power (*jabarut*) and the angelic realm (*malakut*). According to the Koran: "The heart does not lie in what it sees." (LIII:11) (SS 569)

The Gnosis of the Heart

Gnosis of the attributes of the heart is difficult, as is the description thereof, because of its constant turning (*taqallob*) through the changes of states and advancement through the degrees leading to perfection. This is why it is called *qalb* (that which turns).[1] Since states are divine gifts, which are limitless in number, the turning and advancement of the heart through the degrees leading to perfection and the stages of the pre-eternal

1. The same arabic root (*q-l-b*) as *taqallob*.

Beauty and the Majesty are infinite in number, as well. Accordingly, its attributes and states cannot be confined within the limits of number or be quantified within the bounds of limitation. Whoever speaks in terms of enumeration and limitation, if he truly contemplates the matter, will know that only the determination (*ta'ayyon*) of the limits of perception and the understanding within the confines of one's aptitude can be brought to light.

Several thousand divers have plunged into the ocean of the heart's gnosis, and not one has plumbed its depths or fathomed its wonders and marvels. No one who has encountered any trace of it has understood anything from that trace, nor comprehended the proper value of the pearls that have fallen into their hands therefrom.

'Ali ebn Sufi said, "Everyone freely talks about the heart; if only I might see someone who, in describing the heart for me, might tell me what and how it is."

Now, one should know that when one speaks of the heart, one means that entity from which the cycle of existence has been set into motion and through which perfection is attained. Furthermore, the mysteries of pre-eternity and post-eternity are joined together therein. One who first comes to look into it will ultimately find vision through it. The beauty and majesty of the countenance of the Subsistent are displayed to it. The throne of the Merciful, the waystation of the Koran and the Criterion (*forqān*), the intermediate realm between the Unseen and the visible, the spirit, and the *nafs*, the confluence of the seas of the realm of sovereignty (*molk*) and the angelic realm, the gazer and the gazed upon of the King, the lover and the beloved of God, the bearer and the borne of the mystery of the trust (*amānat*) consigned by God to man, and the Divine Grace, all are attributes of the heart.

The purpose of the marriage between the spirit and the *nafs* is to bring the heart into existence. The aim of the relationship between the realm of sovereignty and the angelic realm is to provide a field for its beholding and a site for its contemplative vision (*shohud*). Its form is shaped from love itself and its insight is illumined by the light of witnessing (*moshāhada*). When the *nafs* was separated from the spirit, love and strife appeared between them; then out of the mating of the two was born the form of the heart. It appeared as a barrier between the sea of the spirit and that of the *nafs*, standing at the meeting point between the two, so that if the two threaten to infringe upon each other, it will prevent this. According to the Koran: "There is a barrier between them. They do not infringe [upon one another]. (LV: 20)

The form of the heart has appeared from love itself so that wherever it sees any sign of beauty it mixes with it. It is never without an object of contemplation, an object of love or a Beloved. Its very existence is founded on love, and the existence of love is through it. In a person's existence, the heart serves as a representation of the throne of the Merciful. The Throne is the greater heart in the macrocosm, and the heart is the lesser Throne in the microcosm. All hearts are subsumed in the throne, just as the individual spirits are subsumed in the Supreme Spirit and the individual *nafs* in the Universal Soul.

The heart has a form and a reality as does the Throne. The heart's form is that of a pine-cone-shaped piece of flesh situated on the left hand side of the body. Its reality is that Divine subtlety mentioned above. Between this reality and its form stands the rational *nafs* (*nafs-e nāṭeqa*) and the animal spirit, for the reality of the heart is pure subtlety and its form pure grossness, and there can be any no relationship between its absolute subtlety and absolute grossness. The rational soul and the animal spirit have two aspects, one facing the realm of subtlety and the other the realm of grossness. They stand between the outward form of the heart and its inner reality, so that each thing produced by the reality of the heart reaches the soul first, accepting it through its subtle aspect and passing it on to the animal spirit through its gross aspect. By the same token, the animal spirit receives each thing through its subtle aspect and passes it on to the form of the heart through its gross aspect, from which it is carried into every corner of the body.

The emanating grace of the mercy from the plane of Divinity flows upon the inner reality of the Throne, from where it reaches the bearers of the Throne; through these it joins the form of the Throne itself, from whence it passes on to the invisible realm. The outer form of the Throne is related to its reality, so that every emanation of grace from that reality may reach the visible realm. First, it reaches its form, from which it proceeds to permeate other bodies. The form of the heart is linked to the reality thereof in the same way. All hearts receive grace from the Throne. The reality of the heart proceeds from the reality of the Throne, and the form thereof from its form. This occurs when the heart encounters the Throne through its attention to God. No created being is more magnificent than the Throne. The Koran refers to its magnificence in the following terms "And He is Lord of the Magnificent Throne." (IX:129) (MH 97)

The Nafs and the Heart Compared

The *nafs* desires multiplicity and the heart unity.

For the gnostic, the *nafs* is the doorkeeper of the heart, standing watch and in service, whereas the heart is the site of presence, the bearer of lordship, and the minister of the dominion.

The *nafs* is absent from God, while the heart is present with Him.

Experiencing pleasure is an occupation of the *nafs*. Since the heart is in presence, it is illicit for it to desire created being. Until the *nafs* is cut off from created being, it cannot be purified, for God is pure and loves the pure.

The Heart as the Frontier between Unity and Multiplicity

The heart is the battlefield between Unity and multiplicity, the two forces battling to dominate the field. If it is contaminated with multiplicity, it becomes foul, while if it falls under the sway of Unity, it becomes pure.

Rumi expresses this in a particularly eloquent way:

God has said,
"My attention is on the heart,
Not the form,
for that is just water and clay."
You say, "I too
have a heart,"
The heart is above
the Throne, not below.
In the dark clay for certain
there is water also,
But it is not proper to do
ablution with that water
Because, though it is water,
it is overwhelmed by clay;
So, do not say of your heart,
"this too is a heart."
The heart that is more sublime
than the heavens
Is that of the friends of God
or the prophets.
It has been fully developed
and made complete.
It has abandoned clay

and come to the sea;
Released from the prison of clay,
it has become the sea.
Our water remains
imprisoned in clay —
O! Sea of Mercy,
draw us out of clay!
The sea says, "I draw
you into myself,
but you keep on claiming
to be fresh water.
Your claim holds you back;
let go of
That notion and come
into me.
Water in the clay of the body
seeks to enter the sea,
But clay clogs its progress
and drags it back.

MM III 2244-2254

The Intellect and the Heart Compared

Through God's turning (*taqallob*), the heart (*qalb*) revolves through promptings, attributes, and states. For this reason, one may say that the heart becomes turned (*taqlib*) through promptings. According to the Koran: "Indeed therein is a reminder for one who has a heart," (L:37) inasmuch as it is turned over in undergoing change of form and attributes. This reference was made to the heart and not to the intellect. The intellect tied to individual notions by its limits of understanding, circumscribes God's commands, which are not to be limited. This is in contrast to the heart, which is the site of Divine theophanies. In the forms of those theophanies it becomes turned, coming to remember what it has forgotten. Here the heart remembers what it possessed before its appearance in the physical form and hence what it has lost. As the Prophet stated; "Wisdom is The only goal of the believer."

One should be aware that between the heart (*qalb*), acceptance (*qabul*) and ability (*qābeliyat*), there is both a spiritual and anagrammatical relationship. The spirit involves the ability to accept forms of all theophanies. The anagrammatical is where if the root letters of *qalb* (heart) *q-l-b* and *qābel* (able) *q-b-l* are transposed, they become interchangeable, thus reflecting the interrelationship between the two. If we read the term *qalb*', as *taqlib* (turning over), a development of the same Arabic root *q-l-b*, its turning over becomes acceptance (*qabul*; root *q-b-l*) and ability (*qābeliyat*, root *qbl* as well).

Now '*aql* (intellect) is a word connoting binding, connection or tying down, the prerequisite of which is to be limited. The reality of remembrance (*dhekr*) through God and in God is free of all limitations and thus incompatible with intellect. The situation is such that this limitation or binding first of all appeared in the First Intellect where it comprehended the light of theophany of the Absolute by its own particular limited aptitude or capacity. For this mystery to be made manifest, there is a limit which God has established. Thus, the reality of the intellect is limitation of the lights of the Absolute. God told the First Intellect, "Write!" That is to say that it should circumscribe and gather together the knowledge of God in his creation till the Day of Resurrection. This is the limitation leading to the ultimate limitation. Acceptance of all theophanies is only possible for the essential reality of humanity, that which is concentrated oneness and pre-eternally and post-eternally perfect. This, in reality, is the heart of the Being of God and the meaning behind all remembrance (*dhekr*). (NN 204-5)

The Heart and the Throne Compared

The prophet stated, "The heart of the believer is the Throne of the Merciful."[1] One should be aware that just as in the universe the Throne is the site of the manifestation of the Name, the Merciful — "the Beneficent, established on the Throne" (XX: 5) — so is the human heart established in one's inward being, equally manifesting the name, the Merciful. At every instant, God manifests in the believer's heart in a different way. However, the manifestation of the Divine perfection appears more in the heart than on the level of the Throne for it serves as a bridge between the Unseen and the visible; it alone embraces the dictates of both realms. Thus the heart is the Supreme Throne ('*arsh-e a'ẓam*).

In view of the saying, "The heart of believers is held between two fingers of the Merciful [namely the Beauty and the Majesty]; He turns them about as He wills."[2] The heart is perpetually in motion, like the Throne.

1. *Traditions*, Vol. I, p. 74.
2. *Traditions*, Vol. II, p.12.

The rank of Divinity constantly seeks to manifest itself and does so through Beauty and Majesty which serve as both the inward and outward manifestations of "Every day He exerciseth (universal) power" (LV: 29). Perpetual motion arises from this desire to manifest through the various divine and spiritual realities (*ma'nā*). (SGR 169-70)

The Throne of the rule
of God's Essence is my heart,
Just as the Glorious Throne
is the Throne of the Merciful.
Maghrebi

The Heart and the Rational Soul Compared

The heart is the form of the level of Unicity (*wāḥediyat*) and the spirit that of Oneness (*aḥadiyat*). If the rational soul (*nafs-e nāṭeqa*) enjoys essential gnosis of God, it is referred to as the spirit, deemed to be equivalent to the First Intellect; while if it has cognition in differentiation, it is termed the heart and deemed to be equivalent to the Universal Soul (*nafs-e kolliya*). (RSh II 197)

The Witnessing, Sound and Contrite Heart

Jorair Baghdadi, an eminent gnostic, said, "There are three categories of heart: the witnessing (*shahid*), the sound (*salim*), and the contrite (*monib*)."

The contrite heart refers to the one "Who fears the Beneficent inwardly and comes with a contrite heart."(L: 33). Every devoted one who fears and is conscious of his faults and turns to his Lord possesses a contrite heart.

The witnessing heart is the one described in the following terms: "Indeed, therein is a reminder for one who has a heart or gives ear and who is witnessing." (L: 37) This indicates that this message which God has given and this gate which He has opened represent God's reminder that the devoted one has a heart and an ear to hear, that this heart has become present with Him.

The sound heart is the one described in the passage that speaks of "one who brings to God a sound heart." (XXVI: 89) Happy the one who has a sound heart! — a heart that is purged of doubt, is constantly with God, is released from the world and the creation, and is liberated from what is other than God.

The sound heart accepts whatever is offered to it and is content therewith. As for the contrite heart, it is the motherlode of pain. Neither does it accept anything, nor is it content with even the richest vestment. The sound heart is possessed by one at the station of grace, while the contrite one is at that of limitation. The contrite hearted are the pain-afflicted on the Path, those who have plunged to the depths of the sea of poverty and are lost to all. Though it be decked with all the rich vestments that exist in the two worlds, as each moment comes, it feels ever more naked. If the whole universe were turned into a banquet and presented to the contrite heart, it would spurn that sumptuous spread, not even tasting it. (KAM VII 128)

The Aspects of the Heart

That the heart is more vast than God's mercy is a fact worthy of wonder and something to be contemplated. If one fully understands this, one should make use of whatever this understanding is worthy of being used.

One should be aware that the heart possesses five aspects: that which stands face to face with God and between which there is no intermediary; that which is adjacent to the realm of spirits, whence it receives from its Lord that which it is capable of recieving through the spirits; that which is particular to the imaginal realm, drawing benefit therefrom to the extent of its relationship to the station of Concentration *(jam')* and in terms of the equilibrium of its constitution, its character, and the ordering of its states in its powers, presence and gnosis; that which is on the level with the visible realm, being particular to the Names, the outer (*aẓ-ẓāḥer*) and the Last (*al-Ākhar*); and the all-encompassing (*jāme'*), which is particular to the Oneness of Concentration (*aḥadiyat-e jam'*), being the level which comes after the level of Divinity (*howiyat*) and being characterized by primacy, finality, outwardness and inwardness.

Each aspect has a site of manifestation in the human realm. The form of the heart of concentration and being (*wojud*) is the Prophet, for his station is the point in the middle of the circle of existence. The five aspects of the Prophet correspond to each realm, plane or level, being connected to the dictates of each respectively, and being manifested with the characteristics of each as indicated above. (NN 200)

The Kinds of Heart

The Prophet stated, "There are four kinds of heart: the pure, illuminated kind in which a lamp has been lit, this being the heart of the believer; the black, upended heart, being that of the infidel; the suspended one, wavering between infidelity and faith, being the heart of the hypocrite; and the two-faced one, with one face directed towards the site of faith and another towards the site of hypocrisy. Succor comes to its faith from the realm of sanctity and piety, analogous to a plant which is purified with the aid of water, while its infidelity is bolstered by the realms of wickedness, analogous to an ulcer which is aided by festering pus. Ultimately, whichever predominates governs it."

The difference between these four types lies in the heart being the product of both the spirit and the *nafs*, being pulled at from both sides. The spirit wants to pull the *nafs* to its realm, and vice-versa, and they are constantly involved in the battle. Sometimes the spirit is dominant, drawing the *nafs* out of its lower center up to the spirit's higher station. Sometimes the *nafs* prevails, dragging the spirit down from the heights of perfection to the depths of error. The heart always follows the dominant side until the domain of one's being has become fully established in one or the other, in which it will then settle.

This situation involves regular alternation between bliss and misery. If post-eternal bliss and pre-eternal favor arrive, the spirit is strengthened and overwhelms the *nafs* and its army, becoming released from this struggle in the process. The spirit ascends from the low point of the creation to the high point of Eternity, turning completely away from *nafs* and heart towards witnessing (*moshāhada*) of the plane of Majesty. Moreover, the heart in following it advances from the station of the heart, at which turning (*taqalloq*) is requisite, to that of the spirit, settling where the spirit is established, analogous to a child following its father. Then the *nafs*, following the heart also like a child, emerges from the site where it has been established, the realm of material nature, and proceeds to the station of the heart.

Such a heart is that of a believer in whom there is not a particle of polytheism or infidelity. God forbid, if the situation should be the reverse of this, the effects of pre-eternal misery and wretchedness would obtain, leading the spirit astray and aiding the *nafs* in gaining strength. The heart would draw the spirit to its own realm; the spirit would descend from its station to the site of the heart; the heart would proceed from its station to the site of the *nafs*; and the *nafs* would descend to and become rooted in the ground of material nature. Such a heart becomes an infidel's heart, one which is upended, plunging into the darkness of infidelity. If no particular aid comes from either side and the pull in both direction remains, but with the side of the *nafs* being strong, the heart wavers in the middle, though being inclined towards the *nafs*. This is the heart of the hypocrite. If the side of the spirit be stronger, or if the pull from both sides is the same, the heart is more inclined towards the spirit, or neutral with respect to the two sides and both faith and infidelity exist therein. This is the two-faced heart, one containing faith and the other hypocrisy. (MH 99)

Hātem Aṣamm said, "The heart is of five kinds: that which is dead; that which is sick; that which is heedless; that which is veiled; and that which is sound. The dead heart is that of the infidel, the sick that of the sinner, the heedless that of the unsuccessful, the veiled that of evildoing: 'They say: Our hearts are hardened' (II: 88), and the sound heart is that which is aware in going about its affairs, steeped in devotion and fearful of the Majestic King." (TA 301)

Sari Saqaṭi said, "Your tongue is the interloper of your heart, and your face the mirror thereof. On your face is found that which is in your heart."

He also said, "There are three kinds of heart: that which is like a mountain that cannot be moved; that which is like a tree, the roots of which are firm but which may be shaken from time to time by the wind; and that which is like a feather, being blown wherever the breeze wishes."

He further said, "The hearts of the virtuous are connected to finality and those of God's intimates to primacy." That is to say, the virtues of the righteous are the vices of the intimates, in the sense that virtue becomes a vice when one receives satisfaction through it, and whatever satisfies arrests development.

The righteous are those who have settled themselves on the bounties of heaven, as indicated in the Koranic verse, "Indeed, the righteous will verily be in ease." (LXXXII: 13) Therefore, their hearts will be connected with finality. On the other hand, the eyes of the advanced, who are God's intimates, are focused on pre-eternity, whereby they will never settle themselves on anything less than that which, in fact, they will never attain.

> Therefore, since they do not settle themselves on anything, they must be dragged to heaven in chains. (TA 338)

The Spiritual Levels of the Heart

The heart comprises seven spiritual levels: the breast (*ṣadr*); the heart (*qalb*); the site of love of creation; the site of vision; the site of love of God; the core of the heart (*sowaidā*); and the innermost core of the heart (*mahjato'l-qalb*).

I. The Breast

> The first of the spiritual levels of the heart is said to be the breast *(ṣadr),* which forms the dividing line between the *nafs* and the heart. Some consider the breast to be linked to the *nafs,* calling it also the understanding *(ru').* This is the view taken by Bābā Rokhā Shirāzi, when he says, "The term, understanding, generally signifies the *nafs*." In Sufi terminology it is this aspect of the nafs which is closest to the heart, which one school of Sufi thought terms the breast. (NK 35)

One school of thought considers the breast to be a level of the heart, such being the case with Najmo'd-Din Rāzi, who writes:

> The first spiritual level of the heart is termed the breast, which is in the motherlode of the jewel of Islam, as indicated in the Koranic verse: "Is one whose breast God has opened up for Surrender unto Him, so that he follows a light from his Lord ...?" (XXXIX: 22) Whenever one finds oneself barred from the light of Islam, it is the motherlode of darkness and infidelity that obtains, as in the passage: "But one who opens the breast to infidelity." (XVI: 106) It is the site of Satan's temptations and the *nafs*' enticement, which tempt "the breast of mankind." (CXIV: 5) Being only the outer shell of the heart, the veil constitutes that part of the heart which is no more than the site of Satan's temptations and the enticement of the *nafs,* which cannot penetrate into the interior of the heart, for it is God's treasury and is the firmament of God's Attributes. Temptations have no access thereto, because "We have guarded it from every outcast satan." (XV:17) (ME 195)

It has been said that the breast is to the heart as the white of the eye is to the pupil. It is the site of entry of temptation, plagues, lust, desires and needs, being the domain under the command of the commanding *nafs* (*nafs-e ammara*), as well as the place where the knowledge of God's decrees and communications are heard. It is called the breast, *ṣadr* (fore-part), because it covers the heart, being the part first encountered.

When Ebn 'Aṭā' was asked how soundness of heart might be gained, he replied, "By first becoming aware through the truth of certitude (*ḥaqqo'l-yaqin*), which is the Koran. Thereby one will be granted the knowledge of certitude (*'elmo'l-yaqin*), after which the vision of certitude (*'aino'l-yaqin*) will be revealed and soundness of the breast will come. The indication of this is that one becomes content with God's ordainment; whether God conveys dread or love, one sees Him as the Preserver and the Guardian, and neither blames Him nor protests." (LT 226)

Once there was patience in the veil of my
heart, now it is gone;
Love has set fire to the platform
where that patience once stood.
MM VI 4161

II. The Heart Itself

The heart itself, as the second spiritual level of the heart, is the source of all faith, as indicated in the verse: "He has inscribed faith in their hearts." (LVIII: 22) It is also the site of the light of the intellect: "And have they not hearts with which to feel..." (XXII: 46), and the locus of insight: "For, indeed, it is not eyes that grow blind, but hearts, that are within breasts, that grow blind." (XXII :46) (ME 196)

It has been said that the heart within the breast is like the darkness of the pupil of the eye amidst the white. It is the site of the light of submissiveness (*khoshu'*), purity, love, contentment, certitude, fear, hope, patience and satisfaction, with sufficiency, as well as being the source of the principles of knowledge. The heart is to the breast as water is to a pond. The heart is the root, or principle, and the breast the branch, or corollary.

In the Koranic passage where Moses says, "My Lord open my breast," (XX: 25), Moses wanted the veil of his breast to be opened rather than the heart itself because constriction affects the breast not the heart. The breast, is one thing, the heart another. The breast receives information, while the heart sees. The breast stands in awe; but how could the heart be constricted, when it is gladdened by witnessing (*moshāhada*) in constant intimacy (with God) and by the pleasure of vision and the fruits of witnessing? (KAM VI 134)

III. The Site of Love for the Creation

The site of love for the creation (*shaghāf*)[1] is the source of loving-kindness and love and compassion to created beings, as indicated in the passage, "Indeed, he has smitten her to the heart with love;" (XII:30) the love of created being is particular to the site of love for creation (*shaghaf*). (ME 196)

Esmā'il Ḥaqqi Brusawi, author of the Koranic exegesis, *Ruḥ al-bayān*, reverses the conventional order with respect to the site of love for creation and the site of vision, seeing them as respectively the fourth and third spiritual levels of the heart. He writes:

The third layer is the sight of vision being the pavilion of witnessing (*moshāhada*) God, as indicated in the Koranic passage, "The heart does not lie in what it sees." (LIII:11) The fourth layer is the site of love for creation, enveloping the way-station of love (*'eshq*), as indicated in the verse: "Indeed, he (Joseph) has smitten her (Zolikā) to the heart with love." (XII: 30)

When the Lord of the Worlds wishes to draw the quarry caught in the lasso of grace into the way of religion, He first casts a glance into the quarry's breast to purify it of the passions and of contrivance (*bed'at*) and set its steps straight upon the road of the custom (*sonnat*). Then He casts a glance into the quarry's heart to purify it of the world and of blameworthy characteristics, such as conceit, envy, arrogance, hypocrisy, greed, animosity and thoughtlessness launching it on the way of virtue. Then He casts a glance into the quarry's vision, bearing it off from created being and attachments, opening the eye of knowledge and wisdom in the heart, and making the light of His guidance His special gift. The Koran states that "he follows a light from his lord." (XXXIX: 22) Then God casts a glance into the quarry's love for creation, bearing it off from materiality and setting its feet in the lane of annihilation. (RB VIII 97)

1. The word for enamor *(shaghaf)* comes from the same Arabic root *(sh-gh-f)* as that for pericardium *(shaghaf)*.

IV. The Site of vision

The fourth spiritual level of the heart is called the site of vision which is the source of witnessing (*moshāhada*) and the site of viewing (*ro'yat*), as indicated in the Koranic verse: "The heart does not lie in what it sees." (LIII: 11) (ME 196)

It has been said that the site of vision is like the dark center of the pupil of the eye, being the site of Gnosis and the locus of viewing. Site of vision is at the center of the heart, as the heart is at the center of the breast.

He was unaware
that without God's turning
The intellect and site of vision
would be inanimate.

MM IV 3728

Pure viewing (*ro'yat*) is exclusive to the site of vision coming after the veils of stations and states have been lifted and after one has ascended the ladder to the ultimate nearness [to God]. According to the Koran: "The heart does not lie in what it sees." (LIII: 11)

The prophet stated, "I have viewed my Lord."

The gnostic said, "The site of vision contemplates the Essence alone, undiverted." (MA 221)

IV. The Site of Love of God

The site of love of God (*ḥabbato'l-qalb*) is the source of loving-kindness (*maḥabbat*) from the plane of Divinity (*oluhiyat*), which is particular to the true elect, and which cannot contain love of any created being. (ME 196)

VI. The Core of the Heart

The core of the heart (*sowaidā*) is the source of visionary disclosure (*mokāshafa*) of the Unseen and of Divine Pre-essential Knowledge (*'elm-e ladonni*), as well as the source of wisdom, the treasury of Divine Mysteries, and the site of knowledge of the Names, as indicated in the Koranic passage, "And He taught Adam all the Names." (II: 31) Within it are revealed the kinds of knowledge that are denied the angels. (ME 197)

VII. The Innermost Core of the Heart

The innermost core of the heart (*mahjato' l-qalb*) is the source of the lights of theophanies of the attributes of the Divinity (*oluhiyat*). The mystery of "And indeed We have honored the children of Adam" (XVII:70) is that this kind of honoring (*karāmat*) has never been conferred on any other being. (ME 197)

Certain Sufi masters maintain that the spiritual levels of the heart are fourfold: the breast (*ṣadr*), the heart properly speaking, the site of vision, and the site of vision of God (*lobb*). They say of the site of vision of God, that it is the source of adherence to Divine Unity (*tauḥid*), as indicated in the Koranic passage, "Indeed therein is verily a reminder for possessors of the love of God." (XXXIX: 231) They add that the location of the site of love of God is within the site of vision as the light of sight lies in the eye.

The heart has five layers: the breast as the site at which Islam is pledged; the heart itself as the site of the light of faith; the site of vision as the site of God's attention; the inner consciousness (*serr*) as the repository for the treasure of sincerity; and the site of the love of creation as the way-station of Love. (KAM V 59)

Dreams and Visions Relating to the Heart

At the stage of the heart, different expressions of spirit, purity, light and luminescence make their appearance. The innate praiseworthy temperament and fundamental laudable attributes are seen in the forms of rich mines and rare jewels. For example, if one sees silver, it represents veracity; if gold, sincerity; if pearls, the realities of Divine Unity; if rubies, divine wisdom and true love; if amber, knowledge of stars and the effects of loving-kindness; if crystal, the wisdom of material nature and poetic eloquence; if emeralds, chastity; if lapis lazuli, virtue and piety; if turquoise, worship and devotion; if sapphires, justice; if cornelian, courage; if yellow amber, self-mortification; if iron and steel, inward power; if lodestone, loving-kindness and worthiness; if diamonds, firmness and heart discernment (*ferāsat*), assiduous contemplation, and zeal; if glass, tenderheartedness, reception of the light of theophany and intoxication; if bluestone, subtlety of understanding and purity of mind; if bezoar-stone, repentance and contrition; if gold, eloquence, gnosis and miraculous powers; if jasper, the force of endurance, the tolerance of ascetic discipline, intolerance of self-importance and inward stability; if porcelain, the gnosis of certitude and the watering spot of the visible realities (*'eyān*); if emery-stone, constancy; if dross of lead, satisfaction with sufficiency (*qanā'at*), and renunciation of lust.

It is not necessary to limit the relationship of character traits to symbolic minerals or *vice versa.* In the majority of cases, the ruby, the sapphire and the cornelian represent the heart; yellow amber, the inner consciousness (*serr*); colored glass, the spiritual levels of the heart; minted silver, popularity and fame; gold, dignity, stability and majesty. At the spiritual level of the heart as such, in the early stages, illuminations are manifested, appearing in the guise of sensible things of a fiery nature, such as candles, lamps, candelabra, lantern-shows, torches, useful forms of fire, such as for cooking, though free of smoke and soot, this being the fire of hunger, of ascetic discipline, of remembrance (*dhekr*), of yearning, of love, of ecstasy, and the like.

Now, the candle represents the effect of the light of the *shari'at*, the lamp, the effect of the light of the spiritual Path (*ṭariqat*) or the sublime sensible things of a luminous nature, such as the fixed stars, the moon and ordinary stars. When the purity of ascetic discipline increases, the light of the heart becomes ever more visible, reddening, as one observes the undisguised purity of candle, lamp, fire, and star. This light is luminous through capacity, aptitude, the relative strength or weakness of a given constitution, the soundness or sickliness of the wayfarer's mind, and the dispersion of consciousness.

When the wayfarer becomes a person of purity and vision he witnesses the light of worship and devotion, and of praiseworthy traits and attributes. Such lights are those of ablution, of prayer, of remembrance, of fasting, of paying the poor dues (*zakāt*) of the pilgrimage (*ḥajj*), of recitation of the Koran, of the rosary, of saying "God is greater!" (*Allāho akbar*), of saying "There is no god but God" (*Lā elāha ella'llāh*), of magnifying God's Name, of saying "May God be praised" (*al-ḥamdo le'llāh*) of other forms of devotion, of the entrustment (*amānat*), of asceticism, of trust-in-God (*tawakkol*), of contentment, of yearning, of savor (*dhauq*) of love, of loving-kindness, of sincerity and of other spiritual traits and attributes, manifested in such a way that each light is viewed in a very distinct way from any other. (RN 161)

According to the Koran, "Indeed, therein lies a reminder for one who has a heart or gives ear and is a witness." (L: 37)

The Prophet stated, "Indeed in the human body there is a piece of flesh which, when at peace, brings peace to the rest of the body and when corrupt, corrupts the rest of the body; and that is the heart."

The heart of a person possesses one face directed towards the realm of spirituality and one towards the realm of the body. The heart contains both the corporeal and ethereal realms, and distributes Divine grace received from the spirit.

In the microcosm, the heart is as the Throne in the macrocosm. However, the heart possesses certain characteristics and a nobility which the Throne lacks, namely, that in receiving the grace emanating from the spirit: the heart is conscious thereof, while the Throne is not. This is because the grace emanating from the spirit to the heart is received in the form of attribution, the attributes which the spirit confers being life, knowledge and intellect, so that the heart may perceive it, just as when the sun radiates light, its attribute, into a house, the house becomes illuminated by its light. Thus, the house becomes characterized by the sun in a state of luminosity, whereas emanation of the attribute of mercy reaches the Throne in the form of action and power, not as an attribute. Hence, the Throne abides, while through it the effect of that action and power reaches creation.

Everything exists, but life does not necessarily manifest itself therein. Knowledge and gnosis are characteristics of God. It is as when the sun radiates the characteristics of luminosity upon a mountain, the mountain becomes characterized by the attribute of the sun's luminosity. On the other hand, when action and effect are radiated to the ruby and the cornelian in the motherlode, they do not become characterized by the attribute of the sun's luminosity; rather, through the action of the sun, they are affected by the attributes of ruby-ness and cornelian-ness.

Furthermore, the heart possesses the aptitude, when it is purified through the process of traversing the path, for being the site upon which the characteristics of mercy may be established, just as it has served as the site for the establishment of the attribute of spirituality. When in the course of development, perfection, and attention (to God), it attains perfection, it becomes the site for the manifestation of all the Attributes of the Divinity. All else in the

Universe, however, from the Throne down cannot withstand a single ray from one of the divine lights or one of God's Attributes, as with Mount Sinai, when it collapsed and crumbled.

As to what the heart is, what purification of it means, and when the heart attains the perfection of heart-ness, know that the heart possesses an outer form, as a piece of flesh, but not everyone possesses the reality, or soul of the heart, as indicated in the Koranic verse: "Indeed therein is a reminder for one who has a heart." (L: 37)

The heart may be sound or corrupt. The heart is sound when it is pure, corrupt when it is turbid. The heart is pure when its desires are healthy, turbid when its desires are sickly and deficient.

The eye of the heart enjoys witnessing (*moshāhada*) of the Unseen. The ear of the heart hears the utterance of the Unseen and of God. The nose of the heart scents breezes from the Unseen, and the palate of the heart tastes the savor of loving kindness, the sweetness of faith and the flavor of gnosis. The heart's faculty of touch is the intellect, by which it derives benefit from all intelligible things. Hence, the purification of the heart lies in the health of its senses or faculties.

There is a difference of opinion concerning the treatment of the heart. Some have striven to correct and change their temperament, treating each blameworthy characteristic of the *nafs* with its opposite. For example, they have transformed miserliness into generosity by treating it with altruism; in this way they have turned fury into toleration, forbearance and suppression of anger, and turned greed to piety, renunciation of the world, retreat and detachment. It takes a lifetime for even one attribute to be transformed, and if one relaxes one's control for but a moment, the *nafs* will take over once again. ("The *nafs* is a dragon; who said it is dead?"— Rumi). When one turns to work on another attribute, the first one reactivates.

The Sufi approach is to strive to purify the heart through detachment from the world (*tajrid*), detachment from self (*tafrid*), and attention to God. When the disciple, according to his capacity, has succeeded in becoming detached from outer form and attained inward detachment, in the processes of purifying the heart, he engages in retreat and persistent remembrance (*dhekr*) so that through his efforts, the outward senses cease to be active, thereby cutting off the effect brought to the heart by the plagues of sensible things, for turbidity and veiling of the heart are caused by the engagement of the senses with sensible things.

Once the plague of physical senses is cut off, the plague of satanic temptations and urging of the *nafs* (*hawājes*) which cloud and agitate the heart, remain. One may shut these off only through constant remembrance and the rejection of random thoughts.

Through the light of remembrance and the rejection of random thoughts the heart becomes free of the agitation of the *nafs* and Satan, devotes itself to its states, and discovers the savor (*dhauq*) of remembrance, taking it from the tongue and occupying itself therewith. The virtue of remembrance is that it effaces and removes all turbidity and veiling which Satan and the *nafs* have rooted in the heart. When turbidity and veiling have been reduced, the light of remembrance shines on the essence of the heart in which fear and dread now arise as indicated in the Koranic passage, "Indeed the believers are those whose hearts feel fear when God is mentioned." (VIII: 2)

Once the heart has imbibed remembrance, its hardness is removed, and tenderness and pliancy appears therein, as indicated in the passage, "Then their flesh and hearts become softened to God's reminder." (XXXIX: 23)

When remembrance has become continuous in the heart, it takes control of the heart's domain, rejecting all that is not consciousness of God and God's love, and opening the inner consciousness (*serr*) to meditation (*morāqaba*).

Once the sway of remembrance has fully settled upon the realm of the heart, the heart gains peace and intimacy, becoming fearful of anything else as indicated in the passage: "Those who believe and whose hearts are made peaceful with remembrance of God; it is only through remembrance of God that hearts are peaceful." (XIII: 28) As long as the remembrance of and love for any created thing remains in the heart, turbidity and sickness of heart remain. One must apply the polishing instrument of '*Lā elāha ella'llāh*' (There is no God but God) and the potion of rejecting everything other than God to eliminate this, until the heart becomes ready to receive the imprint of God's Name and thence became characterized by the attributes thereof. At that point no notion of anything other than God remains, all being consumed, and the light of remembrance and the substance of God's name replaces all else.

Majdo'd-Din Baghdādi said:

As long as the heart
is aware of bad and good in the world,
It cannot manage
to handle the bad and good of the world.
Up to now there was one heart
and a thousand notions;
Now there is nothing but 'There is no god
but God.'

At this time, the King of love sends the subjects of His Kingdom down into the city of the heart to occupy the crossroads of the heart, the spirit, and the body. He orders the scene of yearning in such a way that the hooligan *nafs* may be bound with the rope of pain. He tightens the noose of striving around its neck and pulls it into the court of the heart, where, beneath the royal banner of love, he cuts off the head of passion with the blade of remembrance, hanging it from the tree of sincerity. Thieving demons, which were once the cohorts of the *nafs,* hear of this and come to witness the royal judgement. They vacate the city of the body and quit this domain once and for all. All rogues and rascals of the blameworthy attributes of the nafs pick up daggers and put on the white shroud of helplessness and submit in servanthood, saying "O Lord, we have oppressed ourselves; If thou forgive us not and have not mercy on us, surely we are of the lost!" (VII: 23). The King of Love causes all these rogues and rascals to repent and invests them with the robe of servanthood, appointing them to the command of the court of the heart, for they have succeeded in achieving what was desired of them.

When the city of the body has become purified of the tumult of the roguish devils and the agitation of the blameworthy traits, and the mirror of the heart has been cleared of the corrosion of material nature, then one may attain the Hall of the Beauty of Impenetrability and become worthy of the rising place of the sun of the beauty of Oneness.

At this point the heart is governed by the King of Love and the minister of the intellect is the guardian of the door of the heart. The city of the heart becomes adorned with the ornaments, pearls, and the jewelry of certitude, sincerity, trust-in-God, munificence, manliness, chivalry, generosity, liberality, shame, courage, heart-discernment and a diversity of praiseworthy traits and characteristics. What has taken place? The true King has entered the retreat of the heart. The True Beloved displays His beauty as He emerges from the pavilion of the majesty. Now the herald, *'Lā elāha'*, empties the grand hall of even the praiseworthy traits, for God's jealousy negates any otherness. The heart, which is an old burnt-up lover, dwelling like Jacob in a house of sorrows of the breast, finds its eyes illuminated by the beauty of Joseph, turning the house of sorrows into a rose-garden through the beauty of Joseph. It passes from sorrow to joy, from trial to fortune, and from the pain of separation to the preciousness of Union.

At this station, the heart attains its reality and returns to its original soundness and purity. Those attributes of the *nafs* that have not become transformed through a lifetime of spiritual striving become changed through the alchemy of remembrance and the meditation of the heart, its attention entirely fixed on servanthood.

Here, the commands come from neither the heart nor the spirit, and therefore certain traits of the nafs cannot be commanded to comply or not. Rather, the King becomes the one referred to in the Koranic passage, "And faces humble themselves before the Living, the Everlasting." (XX: 111) The King empties the hall of the heart of the burden represented by all that is other than Him, building the throne-room of the elect, where, "Neither My earth nor My sky hear Me, but the heart of My believing servant hears Me."[1] Next, God's command embraces the body and the personal characteristics of the individual, according to, "And God embraced his affairs." (XII: 21) No limb or characteristic can do anything through its own volition; it is only through God's command that one acts, according to "I became [My servant's] ears, eyes, tongue and hands, with which he hears, sees, speaks and strikes."[2]

Thus, at this station, the heart becomes the site of the manifestation of all God's Attributes. Since they are of two kinds, those of grace and those of wrath, and the heart is the site of manifestation of both, God may reveal either to the heart, which in itself is constantly subject to the influence of both. Concerning this, the Prophet stated, "The believer's heart is held between two fingers of the Merciful; He turns it as He wills."[3] This is a reference to the Mercifulness, not to the Divinity, for the heart has become

1. Compare *Traditions*, I, p. 25.
2. *Traditions*, I, p. 15.
3. *Traditions*, II, pp. 12-13.

the site of the establishment of the Attribute of Mercifulness. (ME 187-9)

Purification of the heart involves the cultivation of praiseworthy traits of character, that is, wisdom, chastity, justice, courage, generosity, munificence, liberality, magnanimity, beneficence, grace, chivalry, bestowal, manliness, fidelity, loving-kindness, companionship, kindness, forgiveness, mercy, humility, knowledge, shame, cheerfulness, continence, piety, worship, devotions, and so forth. When the heart becomes characterized by these traits, through the *dhekr, Lā elāha ella' llāh,* polishing clean the corrosion and grime of attachments and obstructions from the mirror of the heart, spirituality, purity, light and luminosity appear. (RN 160)

Correction of the Heart

Correction of the heart involves three things: fear of complacency which might bring destruction, development of the blessing of hope rather than pondering upon despair; and development of freedom of heart rather than dwelling upon the hardship of dispersion. (KAM V 728)

SPIRIT

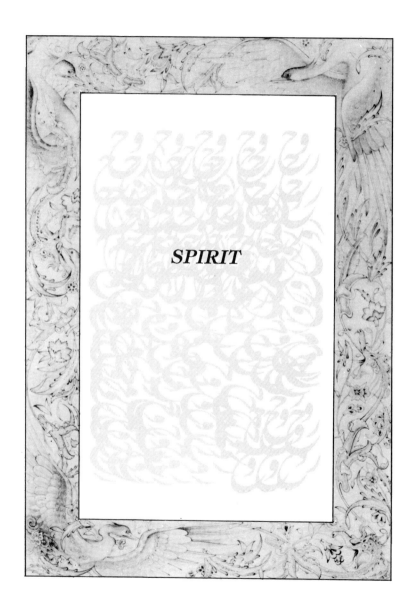

SPIRIT

The spirit to which we now refer is that which is found when the human psyche has taken leave of the spiritual level of the heart and advanced or ascended to a higher realm.

The human heart is the plain that stands between Unity and multiplicity. If it is dominated by the *nafs* and the soldiers of the passions, who constitute the troops of multiplicity the heart is ruined and taken captive. If the army of love, which is the force of the spirit of Unity, expels the troops of the *nafs* from the heart, the heart falls under the influence of the spirit, which becomes its commander. At this station, the psyche of the Sufi becomes linked to the realm of Unity and becomes severed from the world of multiplicity.

The site where the spirit establishes itself in the being of man is the heart. The site of the spirit is that level of the heart that enjoys a viewpoint of the lights of God, where God spontaneously displays theophanies without veils. The heart is an oyster shell and the pearl is the spirit.

When the psyche reaches the level of the spirit, it gains life from the Attribute 'the Living' and becomes the essence of all things through the Attribute 'the Everlasting.'

One whose heart has come alive through
love will never die;
Our longevity is stamped and sealed in the
ledger of the world.

The Spirit as the Site of Love

Friendship comprises three stations: desire, which is an attribute of the body; loving-kindness, which is an attribute of the heart; and love, which is an attribute of the spirit.

Desire arises from the *nafs*, loving-kindness from the heart, and love from the spirit. The *nafs* is not free of desire, nor the heart of loving-kindness, nor the spirit of love. Love is the refuge of the lover, and the lover the refuge of affliction. Love is the torment of the lover, and the lover the torment of affliction.

The love that is the attribute of the spirit is of three categories. The first category is that of truthful love, which is that of the gnostics.

The second category is that of drunken love, which is that of those distracted by love, who are restless and infatuated. Drunkenness may affect either the *nafs*, the heart, or the spirit. When wine overpowers the intellect, the *nafs* becomes drunk. When nearness overcomes awareness, the heart becomes drunk. When revelation overwhelms nearness, the spirit becomes drunk. When the Sāqi is himself revealed, existence begins and drunkenness disappears.

The third category is that of non-being, which is that of those shorn of self, who have pledged themselves to God and have become invisible in both this world and the next. Both worlds pledge themselves to love, and love pledges itself to the Beloved. At this stage they can say neither, "It is I," nor "It is He."
(KAM II 94)

The Levels of the Spirit and of the Heart

The level of the spirit is the shadow of the spirit of Oneness, while that of the heart is the shadow of the spirit of Unicity.
(RSh II 135)

The Adornment of the Spirit

The perfect level of the spirit is adorned with the attributes of Lordship, and is worthy of God's vicegerency. One school maintains that the *nafs* must be refined in order for the spirit to be adorned. Another group maintains that unless the spirit is adorned the *nafs* cannot be refined.

Our view is that even if one spent one's entire life striving to refine the *nafs*, it would still not be completely refined and one would not even have an opportunity to work with the spirit. However, if one makes the *nafs* firm in the etiquette of the Path, concentrating on purifying the heart and adorning the spirit, Divine Graces will appear one after another through the influence of the attraction exercised by the favor and grace of God. Thus, in a single instant, one may acquire a considerable amount of refinement of the *nafs*, which could not be gained through the spiritual endeavors of an entire lifetime. Accordingly, on our Path, refinement of the *nafs*, purification of the heart, and adornment of the spirit begin at the same time, conditioned by the traversal of the Path, so that the wayfarer may arrive at the goal all the sooner.

On the other hand, those who have been utterly slain by the *nafs* remain unaware of the realm of the spirit, and the conditions of traversal of the Path have no effect whatsoever upon their psyche. Just as the *nafs* may enjoin the group who follow this path to lust and corruption, so it may enjoin them to turn to the spiritual Path, whereby they choose a master from among themselves, one who is totally governed by the *nafs*, and who they worship fanatically, demonstrating a devotion to him that is indescribable, for he becomes a manifestation of the *nafs* which they glorify. Whatever action such a master undertakes is considered by his disciples to be an expression of Divine revelation and miraculous powers, through which their devotion to him increases.

> The spirit, like an infant, suckles at the breast of the Path (*ṭariqat*), drinking the milk of detachment from the attachments of material nature, while at the breast of Reality (*ḥaqiqat*) it suckles the milk of infusions from the Unseen, of luminous manifestations (*lawā'eh)* and effulgence of the Divine Lights, so that through the action of infusions and theophanies of spiritual lights the spirit becomes liberated from the bonds of corporeal attachments and released from the prison of human characteristics, to pass on to the frontier of one's pre-eternal state, hearing again God's question: "Am I not your Lord?" (VII: 172) and responding affirmatively.
>
> Once the spirit has emerged from the bonds of human nature and become cut off from the plague of domination by illusion and imagination, everything in the realm of sovereignty (*molk*) and the angelic realm (*malakut*) is at one's disposal, such that one contemplates all God's signs in the particulars of the outer realm, while in the mirror of the inner, one beholds all through the spirit of Unicity.
>
> In this state, if one looks through the window of the senses, one sees everything as an effect of God's signs. An eminent Sufi said, "Wherever I look I see God."
>
> At this point, love has become purified, having shed the veils of the letters of its name. Love and the spirit intermingle, becom-

ing one and the same, as Unity emerges. Wherever the spirit seeks itself, it finds love.

At this station, love replaces the spirit. The spirit becomes the moth of the candle of the beauty of the Impenetrability (*ṣamadiyat),* soaring around the pavilions of the court of Oneness (*aḥadiyat*).

At this station, the graces of Lordship welcome the spirit, ushering it onto the carpet of expansion at this point, commence loving speeches.

When torrents of the wine of God's majesty reach the palate of the spirit, they swirl through all the parts of the spirit's being, such that under the onslaughts of this wine of existence the spirit concentrates on non-existence, turning away from the flourishing oasis of the expression of being towards the devastated wastelands of annihilation.

The spirit lingers for a time at these Heights, this being a waystation[1] between the heaven of the realm of the Divine Attributes and the hell of the realm of material existence, with the vestiges of the attributes of being becoming effaced from the devoted one through the wine of contemplative vision (*shohud*).

With the restraint of the spirit and the overpowering of its yearning by the presence of God along with the action of infusions from the Unseen, miraculous powers of various kinds appear both outwardly and inwardly.

If, at this station the wayfarer eyes these bounties, he is denied the presence of the Bestower thereof. However, if he blinds the eye of his soul with the dust of the Path he becomes worthy of contemplating the signs of the Divine Splendor. This is the threshold where the blood of a hundred thousand sincere ones has been shed in vain.

Many are the truthful wayfarers and seekers who have entered the tavern of ruin of the spirits and become drunk from the cup of miraculous powers, and after imbibing that wine, have fallen into the drunkenness of conceit and self-deception and never awakened to sobriety. They have remained veiled by miraculous powers, making of those very powers the idol of their moment, binding the cincture of self-indulgence around their waists, turning away from God, and devoting themselves to created being.

---

1. The Heights *(al-A'rāf)* is the name of Sura VII, referring to the intermediate realm indicated in the text.See Nurbakhsh, *Sufi Symbolism,* vol. III, London:1988, p.213.

Now, when those who succeed are blessed with the bounty of miraculous powers, they are conscious of the Bestower, not the bounty which is bestowed; they give thanks for the bounty with the eye of the Bestower, so that they become worthy of the Being of the Bestower.

The duty of devotion on the part of the spirit at this station is to serve at this threshold and cease to aspire to anything other than God. Even if one is asked a thousand times what one wants, one replies that one wants nothing, for wanting means being conscious of existence, while we are concerned with nonexistence. Henceforth one cannot proceed on the feet of humanity or strike with the arm of manliness.

At this station, the spirit finds itself overwhelmed with yearning and the distraction of love, such that it grows weary of its own existence, and seeks its own destruction.

While the spirit is being detained at the threshold of divine Might, subjected to the torture of separation and the pain of yearning, the madness of the moth arises within it. In this distress, helplessness and brokenness, the spirit despairs in itself and its dealings [with God], hurling itself about and wailing about God.

When the smoke of the wailing of this burned-up one at the station of distress reaches the presence of the Compassionate, God lifts the veil of Might from before the beauty of divine Impenetrability (*aṣ-ṣamadiyat*) and caresses His burnt-up lover with a thousand graces.

When the candle of the beauty of Impenetrability is displayed in theophany, the moth-like spirit spreads its wings, and the radiation of the candle's attraction steals away the moth's existence. A ray of the light of theophany adorns the moth's being with the ornaments of the candle's attributes. Flaring out, a flame from the candle of the majesty of the Oneness (*aḥadiyat*) consumes the harvest of the moth-spirit so that no chaff remains. (ME 210)

Love is the commander-in-chief of the spirit of Unity. When it pitches its tent in a heart, it routs the hosts of desire and the passions and egocentricity of the *nafs*.

Love is a Divine attraction. When it finds its way into a heart, it dries up the roots of that person's being, linking the heart to Absolute Being.

Love is a tornado that blows up from the land of Unity and sweeps the heart clean of the dirt and grime of multiplicity, carrying it to the realm of unity.

Love appears only in the heart that is worthy of receiving it. The heart is worthy of receiving love when it has defeated all the defenses of the *nafs* through spiritual striving.

Whoever wishes to attain love, must sweep the heart clean of the dust of desire and the passions with the broom of devotion, so that love may accept his appeal.

Preparing the heart for love is the function of the path *(ṭariqat)* and arriving at love is Reality (*ḥaqiqat*).

The heart that lacks love is no heart; love does not settle in just any heart.

In truth, love must come to one; it cannot be learned. However, the heart may become receptive to love if it is purified of the pollution of the *nafs*. Love may enter into a heart that is burnt up, not one that has been dedicated to desire and the passions. Thus, it has been said that love is an attraction which comes suddenly, though only to one who is aware.

A person may spend a whole lifetime struggling with the *nafs* and never be found by love. On the other hand, a burnt-out person may burst out one night with a gasping sigh and be carried away by love. In any case, the point is that not everyone who runs after the prey catches it. But the prey cannot be caught without being pursued.

Love requires a sincere heart and a lover's soul, liberated from all attachments.

Make your outer and inner being one through the power of sincerity and devotion, so that love may enter your heart and bring you to Unity.

As long as you are in the bonds of your self, you are no Sufi, for love does not associate with the *nafs*.

The heart is the domain of the two directions of Unity and multiplicity. When a heart has become purified of the corrosion of multiplicity, the Sun of love causes it to shine with the light of Unity.

Love is the alchemy of Being. One must die to the self in order to gain the treasure of eternal life.

Love is all fortune
and favor,
All opening the heart
and guidance.
Abu Ḥanifa taught nothing
of love;
Neither did Shāfe'i give
an account.[1]

How wondrous is the sura on love;
Before love, the four holy books
do not amount even to a verse.
The law's strictures
last till death;
The science of love
has no end.

Rumi

1. Abu Ḥanifa and Shāfe'i were the founders of two of the four principal schools of Sunni Islamic jurisprudence.

INNER CONSCIOUSNESS

INNER CONCIOUSNESS

When the human psyche is perfected at the level of the spirit it attains the level of inner consciousness (*serr*), which is the site of contemplative vision (*shohud*).

Higher than the spirit, the inner consciousness is the sacred angelic intellect residing in the Divine subtlety which has been consigned in trust to the spirit. Those revelations (*kashf*) of attributes that flow to the inner consciousness from the Divine realm of Reality are perceived by the spirit. It is the site of the spiritual realities (*ma'nā*) of God's knowledge. That which is revealed to the inner consciousness is hidden to the spirit and the heart for it is the hidden things of God's Knowledge which directly affect the inner consciousness without the influence of the spirit. The inner consciousness is subtler than the spirit, which in turn is more noble than the heart.

The gnostic said, "The inner consciousness is the site of the lights of witnessing (*moshāhada*)." (MA 153)

The inner consciousness is that which God keeps hidden, keeping watch over it Himself. (LT 231)

The lover's inner consciousness watches over God's mysteries, which God has called the Unseen, namely, that which is hidden from even the inward eyes, being apparent only to the eye of the inner consciousness.

The gnostic said, "The inner consciousness views revelations of special Attributes in the guise of lights." (MA 126)

Whenever the witness of God enjoys contemplative vision (*shohud*) of God with a purified inner being detached from phenomenal being, he becomes a source of the mysteries of the Names, Attributes, Qualities and Essence. In stability, in gnosis, in constancy in devotion, and with perception of the Lordship. God speaks to him about those pre-eternal sciences and Eternal Knowledge that exist in His Essence. In this situation, the secrets of the decrees from the Unseen become revealed to him, whereupon the eye of his inner consciousness becomes enhanced with the collyrium of the light of God's mystery (*serr*). He looks at God's mystery through God and from God to God's mystery. God's mystery speaks with God's tongue. Then he passes through the inner consciousness to the innermost consciousness (*serr-e serr*) as indicated in the Koranic passage where God spoke through the Prophet with the outward tongue of his inner consciousness and inward nature, saying, "And if you speak aloud indeed He knows the inner consciousness and the innermost consciousness." (XX:7) The innermost consciousness is the ultimate inner consciousness.

Hence, the Prophet has described the chieftains (*noqabā'*) of Reality and the substitutes (*abdāl*)[1] of gnosis as the motherlode of the mysteries.

Certain masters have said that the inner consciousness senses that which the consciousness of the *nafs* cannot sense.

It is recounted that Yusof ebn Ḥosain said, "The hearts of men are the tombs of the inner consciousness." He also said, "If my heart ever learns what has occurred in my inner consciousness, I will tear it out and throw it away." It has been said that the inner consciousness is part of the ultimate inner consciousness that is God, for it is apparent to God alone, while whatever is apparent to created being is not the inner consciousness.

It is recounted that Ḥosain ebn Manṣur Ḥallāj said, "My inner consciousness is virgin, and cannot be revealed by the imagination of anybody."

The gnostic said, "God's actions involve mysteries (*serr*), which have been revealed to the sages. These mysteries are the subtleties of pre-eternal wisdom in the ordering of the forms of phenomenal existence. God possesses mysteries in His Attributes, which are revealed to the gnostics, these being the spiritual realities (*ma'nā*) of the Names which contain gnosis of the decrees of the Eternal. God also has mysteries in His essence,

1. Two ranks of the friends of God. (*auliā'*) see: *Sufi Symbolism*, vol. VI. pp.12-18, 25-26, 51-56.

these being the light of realities that He reveals to the noblest adherents of Divine Unity (*tauḥid*). (MA 157)

The inner consciousness is that level and limit which is specifically bestowed on a given entity at the time of experiencing God's creative Divine Unity. This is referred to in the Koranic passage: "And Our word to a thing if We intend it is only that We tell it: Be! and it is." (XVI: 40)

Hence, it has been said that only God knows, loves, and seeks God, for it is the inner consciousness that seeks, loves and knows Him. As the Prophet stated, "I have known my Lord through my Lord."[1] (ES 100)

The inner consciousness is said to be a matter of the Unseen which is hidden from the intellect.

To know this inner consciousness,
one must pass
From the particular to the universal.
TT 206

One school of Sufis maintains that the inner consciousness is one of the spiritual subtleties at the site of witnessing (*moshāhada*), just as the spirit is a subtlety at the site of loving-kindness and the heart one at the site of gnosis. Another group holds that the inner consciousness is not one of the principal essences (*a'yān-e thābeta*) but a spiritual reality (*ma'nā*), meaning that it is a secret state between the devoted ones and God, of which others are unaware.

They say that between the devoted one and God there is both an inner mystery and an innermost mystery called the most arcane (*akhfā*) as indicated in the Koranic passage: "And if you speak aloud, indeed He knows the inner consciousness and the innermost consciousness." (XX:7) The inner consciousness is that of which only God and the devoted one are aware, while the innermost consciousness is that of which even the devoted one is unaware. God alone is aware of it.

Concerning this first school, which considers the inner consciousness to be an entity in itself, some maintain that it is higher than the spirit and the heart, while others hold that it is higher than the heart, but lower than the spirit. Shehābo'd-Din 'Omar

1. See: *Traditions*, vol. II, p. 34.

Sohrawardi believes that the inner consciousness is not an entity separate from the heart and the spirit, saying that the argument of the school which considers the inner consciousness to be higher than the spirit is that, after the spirit has become completely liberated from the bondage of attachments of the heart and the *nafs*, it is endowed with a different characteristic. They assume that it has become another entity higher than the spirit. What they do not realize is that it is the same as the spirit but characterized by different qualities. The reason for the error of those who have posited the inner consciousness as lower than the spirit, while higher than the heart, lies in the fact that the heart has different characteristics in the final stages of states when it has become fully liberated from the wayward grip of the *nafs* and released from the attachments of the *nafs*' urgings (*hawājes*) and the clinging to satanic temptations.

Some interpret the inner consciousness in yet another way: as a subtle spirituality (*ma'nā*) hidden in the core of the spirit and closed to interpretation by the intellect; or hidden in the core of the heart, the tongue incapable of describing it. (MH 101)

Abu Bakr Wāseṭi said, "The body is completely dark, and its lamp is the inner consciousness. If one has no inner consciousness, one is forever in darkness." (TA 744)

Abu Sa'id Abo'l-Khair recounts that he once asked Pir Abo'l-Fadhl what the inner consciousness was. "You," came the reply. When he asked what the innermost consciousness was the reply was "You, as well." (TA 818)

The eighty-third field is that of the inner consciousness, which derives from the Field of Detachment from Self. According to the Koran: "And God knows their inner consciousness." (XLVII: 26)

The inner consciousness is the quintessence of a person who is with God; it is hidden, so that no tongue can describe it, nor can the individual himself give an account of it. It is of three kinds:

The first is that which is hidden from others, being observance of retreat, which itself involves three things: knowing the condition of service, not violating the rights of others, and preventing oneself from harming others. Retreat is itself an error for whoever does not observe these things.

The second is that which is hidden from the angels, being the revelation of Reality (*ḥaqiqat*); it has three indications: expansion of heart in receiving the Power, not accepting people's justifications for avoiding responsibility with respect to God, and opening one's eyes to God's bounties.

The third is that which is hidden from oneself, being immersion in Union with God, which is a flash of lightning that focuses the eye of the devoted one's heart on God. It touches on three things: fear of one thing, hope of one thing and love for one thing. That one thing is God, and whatever is other than Him is a non-thing and lost. (SM)

Certain masters have considered the inner consciousness and the arcane (*khafi*) to be separate from each other. While in the view of others they are one and the same.

In Sufi terminology, the arcane is a Divine subtely which lies in potential in the spirit, having been consigned there in trust and being actualized only after one has become overwhelmed by Divine infusions (*wāred*). Once this has occurred, the arcane becomes the intermediary between the Divine presence and the spirit in receiving theophany of Divine Attributes and God's emanating grace (*faiḍh*) to the spirit. (TJ 135)

INNERMOST CONSCIOUSNESS

INNERMOST CONSCIOUSNESS

The innermost consciousness is the perfection of advancement of the human psyche, a station at which the gnostics see God through God and only God is aware of this. It is the sea of Unity. At this station, all the drops come together, yet not a drop may be found. It was in this ocean that from Ḥallaj came the declaration, "I am the Truth!", and from Bāyazid came the cry, "Glory be to Me! The highest station is Mine!" Here there is no more news of self or consciousness of self; all is He, from Him and for Him.

The innermost consciousness is that which is exclusive to God, as is the knowledge of both the differentiated and the concentrated realities which are epitomized in Oneness (*aḥadiyat*) and the knowledge of all that is contained in Him or possessed by Him, as indicated in the Koranic passage: "And with Him are the keys to the Unseen; no one knows them but He." (VI: 59) (TJ 156)

The innermost consciousness is that which the spirit of the gnostic senses and takes pleasure in, whereby it becomes exhilarated, and which it cannot demonstrate to the intellect.(SS 574)

The innermost consciousness is the inward aspect of the reality of gnosis. (SS 631)

The inner consciousness (*serr*) possesses an eye which is focused on the innermost consciousness which in turn sees the manifestation of the mystery (*serr*) of the Attributes during revelation of the mystery of the Essence, and this revelation occurs at the point when love leaves the lover.

> The gnostic said, "Viewing the innermost consciousness involves revelation leading to direct observation (*'eyān*)." (MA 127)

> The masters have said that the inner consciousness is that which one may observe, while the innermost consciousness is that of which no one is aware.
>
> The gnostic said, "The innermost consciousness is equivalent to the Ultimate Unseen (*ghaib-e ghaib*)." (MA 154)

Because the reality of the innermost consciousness is hidden from the gnostic, as well as everyone else, it is also called the most arcane (*akhfā*). Ruzbehān says that the most arcane is the same thing as the innermost consciousness. It would seem that the term is derived from the Koranic passage: "And if you spoke aloud, indeed He knows the inner consciousness and what is hidden." (XX: 7)

The most arcane is the highest spiritual level in the advancement of the human psyche.

> Tahānawi considers the innermost conscious to be the spiritual level of the arcane (*khafi*), which is called the most arcane by the wayfarers, and is a light that is subtler than the inner consciousness and the spirit, being close to the realm of Reality (*ḥaqiqat*). This is the subtlest of all the levels of the spirit. It is for the elect alone. (KF 542)

Conclusion

The role of Sufi masters in guiding wayfarers is to strengthen the spirit and its army, which is love, so that the Sufi's heart may be liberated from the grip of the *nafs* and its forces, which are the desires of the *nafs*. In this way the heart may be purified by love and advance to the level of the spirit, the inner consciousness and the innermost consciousness.

BIBLIOGRAPHY

Algar, Hamid, trans. *The Path of God's Bondsmen.*New York, 1982.

Amir Khosrau Dehlawi: See Dehlawi, Amir Khosrau.

Anṣāri, Khwāja 'Abdo'llāh. *Majmu'a-ye rasā'el-e Khwāja 'Abdo'llāh-e Anṣāri.* Ed. M. Shirwāni. Tehran, 1973.

------ *Manāzel as-sā'erin.* Incl. *'Elal-e maqāmāt.* Ed. S. Laugier de Beaurecueil. Cairo, 1962.

------ *Rasā'el-e jāme'-e Khwāja 'Abdo'llāh-e Anṣāri.* Ed. Waḥid Dastgerdi. Tehran, 1968.

------ *Ṣad Maidān.* Incl. *Manāzel as-sā'erin.* Ed. Rawān Farhādi. Kabul, 1976.

------ *Ṭabaqāt aṣ-ṣufiya.* Ed. 'Abdo'l-Ḥayy Ḥabibi. Kabul, 1968.

Arberry, A.J., trans. *The Doctrine of the Sufis.* Partial translation of Kalābādi's *Kitāb at-ta'arrof.* Cambridge University Press, 1977.

----- trans. *The Koran Interpreted.* Oxford University Press, 1983.

------ *Muslim Saints and Mystics.* Partial translation of *'Aṭṭār's Tadhkerat al-auliā'*. London, 1976.

'Aṭṭār, *Diwān-e qasā'ed wa tarji'āt wa ghazaliyāt.* Ed. Sa'id Nafisi. Tehran, 1960

------ *Manṭeq aṭ-ṭair.* Ed. by Seyyed Ṣādeq Gauharin. Tehran, 1977.

------ *Moṣibat-nāma.* Ed. Nurāni Weṣāl. Tehran, 1977.

------ *Tadhkerat al-auliā'*. Ed. Moḥammad Este'lāmi. Tehran, 1975.

Baqli Shirāzi, Ruzbehān: see Ruzbehān Baqli Shirāzi.

Bābā Roknā-ye Shirāzi: See Shirāzi, Rokno'd-Din ebn 'Abdo'llāh.

Bābā Ṭāher 'Oriyān Hamadāni. *Sharḥ-e aḥwāl wa āthār wa dobaitihā-ye Bābā Ṭāher.* Incl. *Sharḥ wa tarjoma-ye kalamāt-e qeṣār, ascribed to 'Aino'l-Qoḍhāt Hamadāni.* Ed. Jawād Maqṣud. Tehran, 1975.

Bākharzi, Abo'l-Mofākher. *Aurād al-aḥbāb wa foṣuṣ al-ādāb.* vol. 2.,

Ed. Iraj Afshār. Tehran, 1979.
Bertels, Yevgeni, Edvardovich. *Taṣawwof wa adabiyāt-e taṣawwof.* Incl. anonymous Persian language MS, *Mer'āt-e 'oshshāq*. Russian text translated into Persian by Sirus Izadi. Tehran, 1979.
Dehkhodā, 'Ali-Akbar. *Loghāt-nāma*. Compiled under supervision of Moḥammad Mo'in. Tehran, 1947-73.
Dehlawi, Amir Khosrau. *Diwān-e kāmel-e Amir Khosrau Dehlawi*. Ed. M. Darwish. Tehran, 1964.
'Erāqi, Fakhro'd-Din Ebrāhim. *Kolliyāt-e 'Erāqi*. Ed. Sa'id Nafisi. Tehran, 1959.
-------*Resāla-ye lama'āt wa resāla-ye eṣṭelāḥāt*. Ed. Javad Nurbakhsh. Tehran, 1974.
Foruzānfar, Badi'o'z-Zamān. *Aḥādith-e Mathnawi,* 3rd ed. Tehran, 1982.
Ḥāfeẓ Shirāzi, Shamso'd-Din Moḥammad. *Diwān*. Ed. Sayyed Abo'l-Qāsem Anjawi Shirāzi. Shiraz, 1982.
Hamadāni, Bābā Ṭāher 'Oriyān, see Bābā Ṭāher 'Oriyān.
Hojwiri, 'Ali ebn 'Othmān. *Kashf al-maḥjub*. Ed. V. A. Zhukovsky. Leningrad, 1926.
Iraqi, Fakhruddin. *Divine Flashes*. Translated by W.C. Chittick and P. L. Wilson. London, 1982,
Jāmi, Abdo'r-Raḥman. *Diwān-e kāmel-e Jāmi*. Ed. Hāshem Rāḍhi. Tehran, 1962.
-------*Haft aurang*. Ed. Mortaḍhā Gilāni. Tehran, 1978.
-------*Naqd an-noṣuṣ fi sharḥ naqsh al-foṣuṣ*. ed. W.C. Chittick. Tehran: Imperial Iranian Academy of Philosophy. 1977.
Jorjāni, 'Ali ebn Moḥammad (al-). *Ketāb at-ta'rifāt*. Ed. Ebrāhim al-Abyāri. Beirut, 1985.
Kāshāni, 'Abdo'r-Razzāq. *Eṣṭelāḥāt aṣ-ṣufiya*. Ed. Moḥammad Kamāl Ebrāhim Ja'far. Egypt, 1984.
Kāshāni, 'Ezzo'd-Din Maḥmud. *Meṣbāḥ al-hedāya wa meftāḥ al-kefāya*. Ed. Jalālo'd-Din Homā'i. Tehran, 1946.
Kermāni, Moẓaffar 'Ali Shāh. *Diwān-e Moshtāqiya*. Ed. Dr. Javad Nurbakhsh. Tehran, 1968.
Khojandi, Kamāl. *Diwān-e Kamālo'd-Din Mas'ud-e Khojandi*. Ed. 'Aziz Daulatābādi. Tehran, 1958.
Lāhiji, Shamso'd-Din Moḥammad, (Asiri). *Diwān-e ash'ār wa rasā'el*. Ed. Barāt Zanjāni. Tehran, 1978.
-------*Mafātiḥ al-e'jāz fi sharḥ-e Golshan-e rāz*. Ed. Kaiwān Sami'i. Tehran, 1958.
Maghrebi, Moḥammad Shirin. *Diwān-e Moḥammad Shirin-e Maghrebi*. Ed. Leonard Lewisohn. London: (forthcoming).

Maibodi, Abo'l-Fadhl Rashido'd-Din. *Kashf al-asrār wa 'oddat al-abrār*. 10 vols. Ed. 'Ali-Asghar Ḥekmat. Tehran, 1978.
Mo'in, Moḥammad. *Farhang-e Fārsi,* 6 vols. Tehran, 1981.
Monawwar, Moḥammad ebn (al-). *Asrār at-tauḥid fi maqāmāt ash-Shaikh Abu Sa'id*. Ed. Dhabiḥo'llāh Ṣafā'.Tehran, 1928.
Moẓaffar 'Ali Shāh Kermāni: See Kermāni, Moẓaffar 'Ali Shāh.
Nāṣer Khosrau Qobādiyāni. *Diwān-e Nāṣer Khosrau*. Incl. *Roshanā'i-nāma* and *Sa'ādat-nāma*. Ed. Mojtabā Minowi. Tehran, 1928.
Ne'mato'llāh Wali, Sayyed Nuro'd-Din, (Shāh). *Kolliyāt-e Shāh Ne'mato'llāh-e Wali*. Ed. Javad Nurbakhsh. Tehran, 1978.
-------*Rasā'el-e Shāh Ne'mato'llāh-e Wali*. 4 vols. Ed. Javad Nurbakhsh. Tehran, 1978.
Nicholson, R. A., trans. *Kashf al-Maḥjub of Al-Hujwiri*. E. J. W. Gibb Memorial Series. Vol XVII. London, 1911; reprint: 1976.
-------, trans., ed. *The Mathnawi of Jalālu'ddin Rumi,* 4th ed., 3 vols. London: Luzac, 1977.
------- *Studies in Islamic Mysticism*. Cambridge University Press, 1921.
Nurbakhsh, Javad. *Farhang-e Nurbakhsh*. 10 vols. London 1984-88.
-------*In the Tavern of Ruin*. New York, 1978.
-------*Traditions of the Prophet (Aḥādith)*. 2 vols. New York, 1981 & 1983.
Pickthall, Marmaduke, trans. *The Glorious Koran*. London, 1930; reprint, 1969.
Qobādiyāni, Nāṣer Khosrau: see Nāṣer Khosrau Qobādiyāni.
Qoshairi, Abo'l-Qāsem. *Tarjama-ye resāla-ye Qoshairi*. Ed. Badi'o'z-Zamān Foruzānfar. Tehran, 1982.
Rāzi, Najmo'd-Din, (Dāya). *Merṣād al-'ebād men al-mabda' ela'l-ma'ād*. Ed. Moḥammad Amin Riyāḥi. Tehran, 1973.
Rumi, Jalālo'd-Din. *Kolliyāt-e Shams yā Diwān-e kabir*. 10 vols. Ed. Badi'o'z-Zamān Foruzānfar. Tehran, 1959.
-------*Mathnawi-ye ma'nawi*. Ed. R.A. Nicholson. Tehran, 1977.
Ruzbehān Baqli Shirazi. *'Abhar al-'āsheqin*. Edited by Dr. Javad Nurbakhsh. Tehran 1970.
Mashrab al-arwāḥ. Ed. Nazif M. Hoca. Istanbul, 1974.
-------*Resālat al-qods*. Incl. *Ghalaṭāt as-sālekin*. Ed. Javad Nurbakhsh. Tehran, 1981.
------- *Sharḥ-e shaṭḥiyāt*. Ed. Henry Corbin. Tehran, 1981.
Sabzawāri, Hādi, (Ḥājji Mollā), (Asrār). *Diwān-e Ḥājji Mollā Hādi-ye Sabzawāri*. Ed. Sayyed Moḥammad Reḍhā Dā'i-Jawād. Esfahan, undated.

Sa‘di, Moṣleḥo’d-Din. *Bustān*. Ed. Nuro’d-Din Irānparast. Tehran, 1977.

-------*Golestān*. Ed. Khalil Khaṭib Rahbar. Tehran, 1969.

-------*Kolliyāt-e Sa‘di*. Ed., Moḥammad ‘Ali Forughi. Tehran, 1978.

Sanā’i, Abo’l-Majd Majdud. *Diwān-e Sanā’i-ye Ghaznawi*. Ed. Modarres Raḍhawi. Tehran, 1975.

-------*Mathnawihā*. Ed., Modarres Raḍhawi. Tehran,

Sarrāj Ṭusi, Abu Naṣr. *Ketāb al-loma‘ fe’t-taṣawwof*. E.J.W. Gibb Memorial Series, No. 22. London, 1914.

Shabestari, Maḥmud. *Golshan-e rāz*. Ed. Javad Nurbakhsh. Tehran, 1976.

Shāh Ne‘mato’llāh Wali: see Ne‘mato’llāh Wali, Sayyed Nuro’d-Din.

Shirāzi, Rokno’d-Din ebn ‘Abdo’llāh, (Bābā Roknā). *Noṣuṣ al-khoṣuṣ fi tarjamat al-foṣuṣ*. Tehran, 1980.

Solami, Abu ‘Abdo’r-Raḥmān. *Ketāb ṭabaqāt aṣ-ṣufiya*. Ed. Johannes Peterson. Leiden, 1960.

Steingass, F. *Persian-English Dictionary*. Tehran, 1978.

Tahānawi, Moḥammad A‘lā ebn ‘Ali. *Kashshāf eṣṭelāḥāt al-fonun*. Ed. Asiatic Society of Bengal. Calcutta, 1982.

Wensinck, A. J. *Concordance et Indices de la Tradition Musulmane,* 6 vols. Leiden: Brill, 1936.

INDEX

Kharrāz, Abo'l-Ḥasan 43
Kharrāz, Abu Sa'id (d. 899) 39
Khawwāṣ, Ebrāhim (d. 904) 31, 41, 82
khoshu', submissiveness 99
Koran 13, 16, 19, 23, 26, 33, 40, 42, 44, 46, 48, 51, 52, 54, 55, 57, 58, 59, 73, 77, 79, 82, 88, 89, 90, 91, 92, 93, 94, 97, 98, 99, 100, 101, 102, 103, 104, 105, 106, 107, 108, 115, 116, 124, 125, 126, 131, 132
- II:251 46
- II:31 101
- II:88 97
- V:54 48
- VII:23 107
- VII:172 48, 58, 115
- VII:199 12
- VIII:2 106
- IX:129 91
- X:70 52
- XII:21 108
- XII:30 100
- XII:108 13
- XII:53 13, 51, 52
- XIII:28 106
- XIV:24 44
- XV:17 98
- XV:29 33
- XV:42 35
- XVI:106 98
- XVI:40 125
- XVII:70 102
- XX:111 108
- XX:25 99
- XX:5 93
- XX:7 124, 125, 132
- XXII:46 99
- XXIV:40 23
- XXV:43 16
- XXVI:89 94
- XXXV:32 55, 57
- XXXVII:164 34
- XXXVIII:43 49
- XXXVIII:72 33
- XXXIX:22 98, 100
- XXXIX:23 19, 102, 106
- XL:54 49
- XLVII:26 126
- L:33 94
- L:37 92, 94, 104, 105
- LIII:11 88, 100, 101
- LIII:14 73
- LV:20 90
- LV:29 94
- LVIII:22 99
- LXXV:2 54
- LXXIX:40-41 48
- LXXXII:13 97
- LXXXIX:27- 28 58, 59
- XCI:7 - 8 57
- XCI:8 13, 26, 57
- CXIV:5 98

Lā elāha 108
Lā elāha ella'llāh, There is no god but God 103, 106, 109
lāhut, realm of Divinity 65
lawā'eh 115
lobb 102
lote-tree 73
Maghrebi, Abu 'Abde'llāh 41
Maghrebi, Abu 'Ali 'Othmān (d. 1154) 43
Maghrebi, Moḥammad Shirin (d. 1400) 82, 94
maḥabbat 101
mahjato'l-qalb, innermost core of the heart 98, 102
Maibodi 53
Majesty 76
makr, deception 13
malakut, angelic realm 82, 88, 115
Mālek Dinār 79
ma'nā, spiritual realities 94, 123,